# Boston

## HISTORY *in the* MAKING

© KINDRA CLINEFF

## By Robert B. Parker

## Art Direction by Jil Foutch

URBAN
TAPESTRY
SERIES

TOWERY
PUBLISHING, INC.

# Boston

## HISTORY

### ∞ *in the* ∞

## MAKING

### By Robert B. Parker

# Contents

Library of Congress Cataloging-in-Publication Data is available on page 317.

# By Robert B. Parker

AWK AND I WERE TAILING A GENTLEMAN, NAMELY
Truly Meadows, who had been dating a
middle aged widow named Inez Lake. The
Standish Bank & Trust suspected him of
conning about two million dollars from Inez, whose recently
inherited trust they managed. They couldn't prove it. Inez
wouldn't admit it. But they noticed that there was two million
fewer dollars in the trust than had formerly been there and
they hoped that I could watch Truly and see if he might lead
me to it. I had asked Hawk to join me, not only because
tailing is much easier for two men than one, but because
tailing is very boring, and Hawk is not.

We had picked Truly up walking down Charles Street at
the foot of Beacon Hill. It was the most Boston of streets
with old brick buildings looking much as they must have
when Paul Revere walked past them. There were antique
shops and restaurants and a variety of other commercial
establishments in the several blocks of it from the area of
Mass General Hospital, to where it ran between The Public
Garden and The Common. We followed Truly along
Charles Street past Toscano restaurant and the old
Lincolnshire Hotel, now an apartment building, down
Beacon past the Cheers bar, along Arlington and into the

Ritz Cafe where he met Inez at a table by the window. She was having a drink already. She jumped up and kissed him when he arrived and he sat down across from her and listened while she talked. Truly was tall, lean, tan, dark haired and handsome. Inez was a bit plump though not hopeless, with too much blonde hair and very expensive clothes that didn't fit right. They shared some martinis by the window, where you could look out across Arlington Street at The Public Garden. There is always argument, even in Boston, about whether it's Garden or Gardens, but a sign hanging at the corner of Boylston and Charles streets reads Public Garden. I went with the sign. The Public Garden is not to be confused with The Boston Garden where the Celtics and Bruins played before it was replaced by the Fleet Center and torn down. Hawk always said it was a no class thing not to call the new arena the Boston Garden. Hawk's a traditionalist.

As we watched, Inez continued talking to Truly who was listening with the attentiveness that two million dollars could command. The Ritz Bar was a dark paneled room with comfortable chairs and tables spaced enough so you could whisper the latest stock quotes to your date. We sat at the bar along the back and had a beer each. Inez continued to talk. Truly nodded.

"Done the bar over," Hawk said.

"Bumpkin," I said. "They did the bar over a long time ago."

"Always liked the old bar," Hawk said.

"Me too," I said, "but when the new folks bought the place they didn't check with me on the renovations."

"Their loss," Hawk said. "Still got a dress code?"

"Yep. And the cafe is still great for a light meal," I said.

"Good to know," Hawk said. "I hate change."

---

Truly and Inez rose as one and moved out of the bar. Truly was still nodding occasionally as Inez talked very intensely about something probably very intense. Hawk went after them. I left a ten on the bar and went after Hawk. They had gone out the side door. Inez and Truly were walking hand in hand up Newbury Street. Truly was nodding.

"Think she'll shop," Hawk said when I caught up with him.

"Women like to shop on Newbury Street," I said.

"I know," Hawk said. "Spent a number of miserable hours standing out front of stores here."

"Anybody ask you to hold their horse?" I said.

"I believe that to be a humor at the expense of my racial heritage," Hawk said.

"I believe it is," I said.

"Thought it was," Hawk said.

Newbury Street runs from Arlington Street to Massachusetts Avenue, the length of The Back Bay. Originally Boston was located on a promontory of land connected to the continent by sort of a goose neck peninsula. In the nineteenth century, the city had shoveled a lot of dirt off of several hills and filled in the body of water behind the city called The Back Bay. The new land was flat as a table top, and very valuable. Developers had built brick and brownstone houses on the landfill which is still called The Back Bay and is some of the most valuable and fashionable real estate in the city. It is bisected the long way by Commonwealth Avenue, which is like a European Boulevard with its wide mall, its trees, and its statuary. Newbury Street parallels Commonwealth Avenue to the Northwest, Beacon and Marlborough streets are parallel to the Southeast. I was hoping that Truly would take Inez on a tour of The Back Bay because it is one of the great urban places in the world

and I always liked walking around there. And because since I lived on Marlborough Street if I lost them, I would at least be close to home. But it became fairly clear that Truly wasn't in charge, and they stuck to Newbury Street.

What Rodeo Drive is to Beverly Hills, or Worth Avenue is to Palm Beach, Newbury Street is to Boston. There are shops and boutiques and salons and emporiums and stores and bazaars and restaurants and bars and places to buy ice cream. Inez went into every one and came out with something, while Hawk and I lounged and watched and blended in with all the other guys lounging and waiting and lingering. Inez worked her way slowly up one side of Newbury Street and back down the other side. Buying and talking. Truly carried packages and nodded.

"Our boy paying for this," Hawk said, as we followed them across the Public Garden toward the Four Seasons Hotel, "then I think I know where the two million went."

"I watched through the front window when she was in Susanna," I said. "Inez is paying."

"Paid for the drinks too," Hawk said. "At the Ritz bar."

"You noticed," I said.

"Yeah."

"And not even a trained detective," I said.

"Trying to be just like you," Hawk said.

"That's good," I said. "Aim high."

Inez and Truly crossed the little suspension bridge over the lagoon and went down the stairs to the Swan Boats. From May to October, pedaled by college aged kids with quads of steel, the big flat bottomed boats with huge swans configuring the bow, moved tourists at a leisurely pace around the lagoon followed by a platoon of ducks begging for peanuts. Susan and I often took a Swan Boat ride,

especially in the transition from late afternoon to early evening with the city rising all around the park, and the light turning violet, and the world seeming a far better place than I know it to be.

"We going to ride?" Hawk said.

"Appealing as it would be," I said, "I think we can watch from the shore."

"Hope they don't jump from the boat and swim for it," Hawk said. "These boots are hand made."

We watched among the squirrels and the Nannies as the boat slowly circled the lagoon. Inez and Truly got out, Truly carrying those of Inez's purchases which were small enough to fit in shopping bags and hence hadn't been shipped. Inez talking. They went across Boylston Street to the Four Seasons Hotel and up to Aujourd'hui, the hotel dining room. The Four Seasons is the best hotel in Boston. The Ritz has its partisans and deserves them. Both offer a grand view of The Public Garden from both Dining Room and lounge. But the Four Seasons feeds you better, and Bob Winter plays piano in the lounge. So I'm a Four Seasons guy—unless, of course, I'm paying my own way, in which case I tend to become a Susse Chalet guy.

"You on expense account?" Hawk said.

"Certainly," I said.

"Then we may as well do something to run it up while we watching them," Hawk said.

It was early in the evening and the dining room was not yet full so we sat on the far side of Aujourd'hui and had supper while they ate and Inez talked and drank wine and paid and she and Truly staggered home with too much wine and all her purchases. Fortunately it wasn't much of a stagger. Inez lived next door in an exotically expensive condo she had bought on

the way home from her late husband's wake.

Hawk and I hung around outside.

"Think she still talking?" Hawk said.

"No reason to think she isn't," I said.

"Our boy really earning his two million if he took it."

By midnight it seemed clear to both of us that Truly wasn't leaving, and that if he did he would not lead us to the money. So we went home to bed.

Truly came out of Inez's condominium at 8:45 in the morning carrying a pig skin briefcase. He was wearing a dandy tan suit, blue shirt, yellow tie and a crisp Panama hat with a big hat band. He paused to light up a large cigar, and set off a brisk pace down around the condominium building to Park Square and through Park Square where the emancipation statue stood, and past it, angling east past the transportation building and onto Stuart Street. We were behind him as he strolled smartly along Stuart Street through the theater district and past Jake Wirth's where they served dark beer and German food. At Washington Street he turned left into Chinatown and went into a small place and sat at a small table and ate Dim Sum and drank green tea. Hawk and I lingered outside, as inconspicuous in the narrow precincts of Chinatown as two tarantulas on a wedding cake.

"Breakfast?" Hawk said.

"I assume."

"So he smoked that rope before breakfast?"

"Seems like."

Hawk shook his head.

"You don't understand about cigars," I said.

"No, I don't," Hawk said. "You?"

"Not really. They have something to do with suspenders," I said.

Truly finished his Dim Sum, paid his bill, and left. Hawk went one way down Beach Street and I went the other so that whichever way he turned we had him covered. He came my way and I stood gazing into a window full of smoked ducks and skinned rabbits and some things I didn't recognize until he reached Washington Street and turned the corner heading downtown. I followed him along Washington Street through the bare vestiges of the now nearly gone Combat Zone where there was still, forlornly here and there an adult entertainment center clinging like the last leaf on a dying tree. Hawk circled the block and picked us up at Bedford Street. The opera house used to flourish at this end of Washington Street and the huge Paramount Theater where Sinatra had played. No more. Bare ruined choirs where once the sweet birds sang.

We went past the disastrous mall they had tried to build in the middle of the city, and past Macy's, once Jordan Marsh, and Filene's, the big department stores that formed the heart of downtown crossing where there was always a lot of street life, and a lot of cops. It was probably the most law abiding place in the city. Further along Washington we passed newspaper row, now gone, where once most of the several Boston Dailies had been headquartered. There were only two left and neither was on newspaper row. Much of Boston resonates with the past, but for all of that, it is a lively and vigorous city, as much new as it was old, and in its best incarnations a nice integration of the two.

At the Old State House, Truly turned down State Street, passed the site of the Boston Massacre and went into a large bank. He disappeared into the safe deposit room while Hawk and I stood filling out deposit slips at different counters and trying hard not to look like bank robbers. Truly came out of the safe deposit room carrying his briefcase. Hawk and I

looked at each other. Hawk formed the word BINGO! I nodded and we followed Truly out past the lobby guard who did not open fire, crossed the street, went down some steps past Fanuiel Hall and into Quincy Market.

Quincy Market was the first of what are now many re-cycled market and warehouse buildings devoted to boutiques, fast food, fashionable booze, and mingling. Three old stone buildings had been rehabbed, brightened, surrounded with cobblestones, amended with some other structures, and thrown open to the public in 1976. More and more the public had come to consist of teen aged kids from the sub-urbs, but there was a genial marketplace quality to the place that I liked.

"You ever come down here," I said to Hawk.

"Every time I want to buy a life-sized ceramic llama," Hawk said.

"Be nice when they get the expressway buried, open it up to the waterfront."

"When you think that going to happen?" Hawk said.

"Two thousand and something," I said.

"Been digging since they shot the brother up there front of the Old State House," Hawk said.

"Crispus Attucks?"

"Un huh," Hawk said. "There go Truly."

Truly had gone in the front door off the central market building, shoved his way through the crowd and suddenly bolted out one of the side doors and was hot footing it across the cobble stones toward the water front. He'd made us, there was no point being covert anymore. We ran after him. He zig zagged through the construction under the still extant central artery and headed for the North End.

"Think we can catch him?" I said.

Hawk looked amused. He was sure that no white guy could run as fast as he could and was always amazed that I could stay with him. Truly had a head start and he was pretty good. We stayed with him without closing the distance as he sprinted down Hanover Street. The North End is Italian. Filled with narrow streets that turn sharply. And on every one of them there was a restaurant, a butcher, a cheese shop and wine store or a place that makes cannoli's. No one had ever starved to death in the North End, though people had died by other means.

Truly skidded around a corner on Hanover Street, took a sharp right onto Fleet Street and was at the waterfront before we got half way down Fleet. Ahead of him was Lewis Wharf, no place to hide. He turned right on Atlantic Avenue and pounded along the waterfront, past the Luxury apartments that had been salvaged from the warehouses left dying after the Yankee Clippers no longer made the run to Canton. He tried to cut through The Marriott and lose us but he went in the wrong door and had to duck out and pick up the pace as we closed. Truly was obviously in shape, and he could really run, but he was carrying a full briefcase which slowed him and we were almost up to him when he turned under the huge archway onto Rowes Wharf and found himself cornered in next to the Boston Harbor Hotel. Hawk and I slowed and walked toward him. He backed down a walkway onto the ferry terminal and then into the little glassed in waiting gazebo with the domed roof. It was empty between ferry runs. And we walked in after him. Past him I could look out the long run of the waterfront as it stretched out into South Boston. The World Trade Center, the fish pier, the old Boston Army base where I had started the process that eventuated in Korea so many years ago. It

was a design center now. The whole waterfront was developing. There was a new hotel and courthouse and big plans for walkways. I was holding to a wait and see on the big plans.

"Who the hell are you guys," Truly said, his chest heaving, and the air dragging into his lungs in big gasps.

"My name is Spenser," I said. "Standish Trust thinks you stole money from Inez Lake, and I think it's in that suitcase."

"What if I won't give it up," Truly said.

Hawk smiled at him.

"Think about it," Hawk said.

Truly stared at Hawk who appeared not to be at all short of breath, though I suspected him of exercising rigorous self control to impress me. I wasn't too winded myself. After a moment Truly handed me the briefcase.

"It's mostly there," he said. "She gave it to me. I didn't steal it. And I only spent a little of it, just for some cigars and stuff."

"Suspenders?" I said.

"Yeah I bought two pair, how'd you know?"

I smiled. Hawk smiled.

"You can probably keep the suspenders," I said. "But you've got to give the dough back."

Truly handed it to me.

"How about Inez," he said.

"I don't think she'll have much interest in you," I said. "Once this is all worked out."

"God," Truly said, "I hope not."

Behind him, across the harbor, a big silver jet plane rose up off the runway at Logan Airport and climbed across the harbor and up over the city and still climbing, while we watched it, disappeared beyond the downtown towers. 🦪

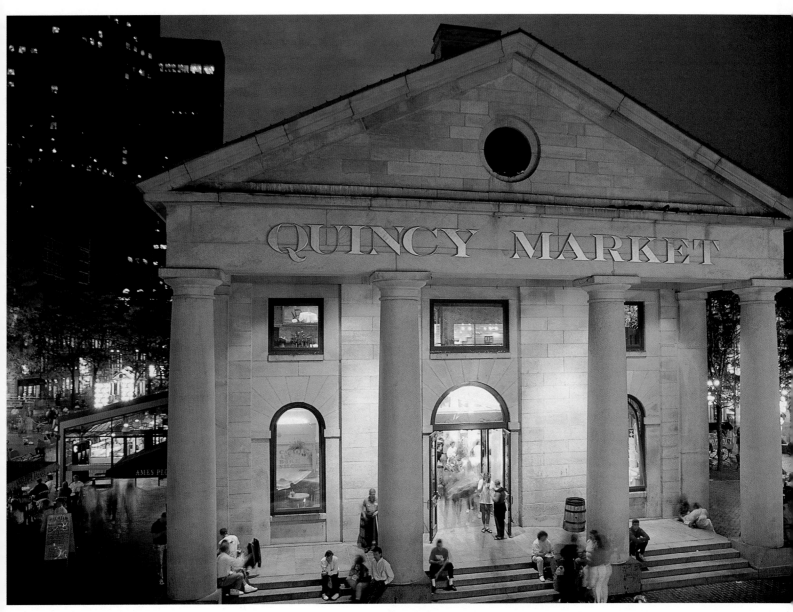

D EVELOPED IN THE MID-1970S, Faneuil Hall Marketplace (OPPOSITE) is an entertainment hub loaded with shops, restaurants, and nightclubs. The thriving mecca of fun combines the centuries-old Faneuil Hall and Quincy Market (ABOVE), both of which were bustling produce, meat, and fish markets in the 1700s and 1800s.

THE SUN SHINES DOWN ON Faneuil Hall, Boston's cradle of liberty. Lovely in all weather, this colonial structure—a 1742 gift to the city from Huguenot merchant Peter Faneuil—originally served as a market and public forum for such patriot activists as Sam Adams. Today, it anchors the Faneuil Hall Marketplace, a complex of shops and restaurants, where—weather permitting—outdoor musicians often play for tips.

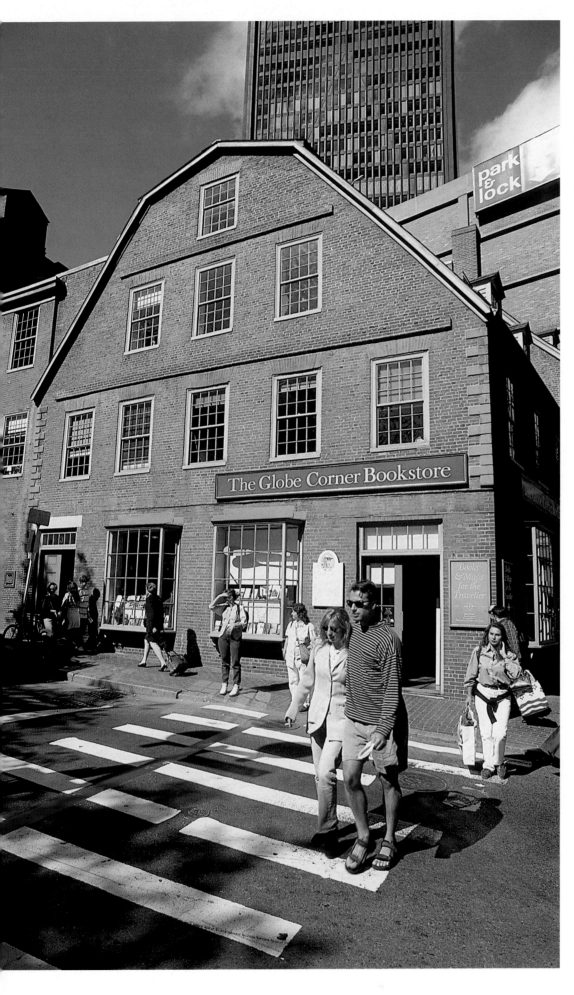

B UILT AROUND 1718, AT THE corner of School and Washington, the historic Old Corner Bookstore building has been many things over the years—an apothecary shop; headquarters to Ticknor & Fields, publishing house for such noted works as *Walden* and *The Atlantic Monthly*; and a pizzeria. Until its recent move, Globe Corner Bookstore called the site home.

T HE OLD STATE HOUSE GLEAMS with ornate elegance against the sleek, postmodernist Exchange Place tower. Once the 18th-century home to the colonial government, the history-embedded site is Boston's oldest surviving public building. James Otis Jr.'s notorious tirade against the Writs of Assistance was made here in 1761, and the Declaration of Independence was read aloud from its balcony in 1776.

Bosto

A BRONZE STATUE OF CIVIL WAR General Joseph Hooker casts a looming shadow on the south lawn at the State House, Charles Bulfinch's architectural masterpiece overlooking Boston Common from Beacon Hill. Its gold-leaf dome an oft-used directional, the building has undergone extensive additions and modifications since its initial completion in 1798.

MOST OF WHAT GLITTERS IN Boston is, indeed, gold, from the Sacred Cod that hovers over the politicos in the State House (OPPOSITE BOTTOM) to the weather vane cricket on duty atop Faneuil Hall (OPPOSITE, TOP RIGHT).

Boston's most elegant garden is at the Isabella Stewart Gardner Museum. A passionate horticulturist, Gardner had her mansion built in the style of a Venetian palace to house her private collection of art, which spans the gamut from modern masters such as Degas and Matisse to works from Dutch, French, Italian, and German masters. Virtually unchanged since its completion in 1901, the museum is the site of a wildly popular Sunday concert series.

THE VIEW FROM THE MAIN stairwell of the Boston Public Library offers a glimpse of *The Muses of Inspiration Hail the Spirit of Light*, one of many ethereal murals that grace this 19th-century Renaissance-style landmark (OPPOSITE). In the city's Financial District, the decidedly modernist John W. McCormack Building and Post Office casts an art deco shadow over the area's narrow colonial streets.

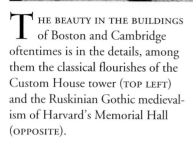

THE BEAUTY IN THE BUILDINGS of Boston and Cambridge oftentimes is in the details, among them the classical flourishes of the Custom House tower (TOP LEFT) and the Ruskinian Gothic medievalism of Harvard's Memorial Hall (OPPOSITE).

Boston

A N ARCHITECTURAL MARVEL from any angle, Trinity Church is one of the most striking buildings in Copley Square. Regarded by the American Institute of Architects as one of the 10 finest buildings in the country, Trinity Church was designed by the renowned H.H. Richardson and completed in 1877.

A LOOMING, 60-STORY MIRROR, the I.M. Pei-designed John Hancock Tower—Boston's tallest building—dominates Copley Square as it reflects the beauty of the city's older architectural monuments, including the Old Hancock Tower, which it replaced in 1975.

F ROM ITS BREATHTAKING
waterfront view at the tip of
Columbia Point to its awe-inspiring
50-foot glass wall, the John F.
Kennedy Presidential Library and
New Museum—another I.M. Pei
creation—is a lavish, lushly land-
scaped tribute to Boston's favorite
political son.

A LONG THE BANKS OF THE Charles River, the town remembers Arthur Fiedler with an aluminum bust near the outdoor stage where he and his beloved Boston Pops Orchestra performed their celebrated Fourth of July concerts (OPPOSITE). In Roxbury, John Wilson's powerful *Eternal Presence* graces the lawn at the Museum of the National Center for Afro-American Artists, which honors the contributions made by African-Americans in the pursuit of freedom during the 19th century.

M URALISTS IN BOSTON PLAY
crucial roles in the celebration of ethnic pride and the awareness of neighborhood concerns.
Known to locals as "Sidewalk
Sam," street artist and instructor
Bob Guillemin (RIGHT) has long
beautified the concrete walkways of
the Back Bay and City Hall Plaza.

BOSTONIANS LOVE A GOOD MEAL, and their passion for food is reflected not just in the bevy of fine eateries, but also in the artful way they advertise their culinary offerings. The giant milk-bottle concession stand outside the Children's Museum is a hard-to-miss landmark of calcium and kitsch.

IT'S HOO

CRABMEAT
SEAFOOD
SALAD

HUMMUS SALAD

TACO SALAD

NEW ENGLAND
·CLAM CHOWDER·

CALZONE
AND
SALAD

QUICHE
AND
SALAD

CHILI

PLEASE THROW
WRAPPERS AND
CIGARETTES IN
PROPER CONTAINER

History in the Making

Boston

W HETHER TAKING COFFEE with your E-mail at the Cybersmith Cafe (RIGHT) or tearing into a plate of ribs at Redbone's (LEFT), Boston restaurants have something for just about every palate. Pink flamingos beckon the hungry into Cambridge-based Magnolias for some top-notch Cajun vittles (OPPOSITE LEFT), while the Blue Diner is a heralded mainstay of the late-night circuit—and a great place to hunker down with a beer (OPPO-SITE RIGHT).

Bostor

T HOUGH RENOWNED FOR ITS clam chowder, Boston nonetheless boasts a slew of ethnic culinary diversions, from Armenian and Portuguese baked goods to bubbling pizza pies to heaping helpings of hearty Mexican.

Some of Boston's most creative people are drawn to the artistry and entrepreneurial excitement of the restaurant business, among them the award-winning chef and author Todd English (OPPOSITE), who owns the immensely popular Figs and Olives eateries. Dining spots such as Clio (TOP) and Mistral (BOTTOM RIGHT) typify the classicism and originality of the Boston culinary scene, while Andrée Robert and her family's Maison Robert (BOTTOM LEFT) have garnered much acclaim for the restaurant's innovative New French menu.

Bosto

© ANDREW BRILLIANT

© ERIC FOWKE

W HETHER CELEBRATING Bastille Day (TOP), shimmying to the music at the Caribbean Festival (BOTTOM), or catching a performance by the Phunk Phenomenon troupe (OPPOSITE), dancing is, as Boston University poet Robert Pinsky once put it, "The expression by the body / Of how the soul and brain respond to music."

T HE BOSTON MUSIC SCENE HAS been attracting international attention for decades, thanks most recently to such hometown favorites as the Mighty Mighty BossTones (OPPOSITE) and The Amazing Crowns (ABOVE), just two groups who've found success far beyond the network of local nightclubs.

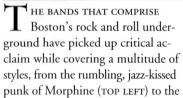

THE BANDS THAT COMPRISE Boston's rock and roll underground have picked up critical acclaim while covering a multitude of styles, from the rumbling, jazz-kissed punk of Morphine (TOP LEFT) to the tough guitar pop of Guster (TOP RIGHT). Both Laurie Geltman (BOTTOM LEFT) and the Gravel Pit (BOTTOM RIGHT) are also fixtures on the Beantown club scene.

Pᴿᴼᴰᵁᶜᴱᴿ ᴬᴺᴰ Cᴼᴹᴮᵁˢᵀᴵᴮᴸᴱ Edison collaborator Brother Cleve (ᴛᴏᴘ ʟᴇꜰᴛ) is Boston's resident lounge guru, while the Gigolo Aunts (ᴛᴏᴘ ʀɪɢʜᴛ) specialize in Beatle-esque power pop. Celtic harpist Deborah Henson-Conant (ʙᴏᴛᴛᴏᴍ ʟᴇꜰᴛ) has perfected a genre-spanning fusion that places the Irish instrument in jazzy-pop settings, and former street singer Mary Lou Lord (ʙᴏᴛᴛᴏᴍ ʀɪɢʜᴛ) has recorded her punk-folk songs for labels across the country.

Boston

THE MURALED MADAME ON
display at Mama Kin, the
Landsdowne Street nightclub formerly owned by Boston rockers
Aerosmith (OPPOSITE), seems to be
influencing the women of the local
club scene, among them Letters to
Cleo vocalist Kay Hanley (LEFT).

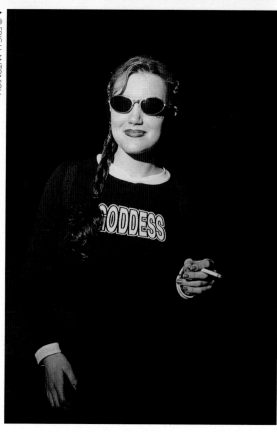

© ERIC H. ANTONIOU

B EYOND THE REALM OF ALTER-
native rock, Boston and nearby
Cambridge both boast thriving
blues and jazz communities populated by ace vocalists, such as
Weepin' Willie (OPPOSITE) and
Shirley Lewis (LEFT).

Tradition and precision are among the hallmarks of the artisans at Verne Q. Powell Flutes, Inc., a Waltham-based company that has been crafting fine flutes and piccolos since 1927 (OPPOSITE). That same craftsmanship is applied by area luthiers (ABOVE).

Bosto

I N BOSTON, ACADEMIA AND THE arts are often intertwined. Acclaimed musician Al Kooper, who played organ on Bob Dylan's "Like a Rolling Stone," teaches at the Berklee College of Music (OPPOSITE). Former U.S. poet laureate Robert Pinsky is an instructor in the graduate writing program at Boston University.

FEW WOULD DISAGREE THAT local authors Doris Kearns Goodwin and Andre Dubus have the "write" stuff. A presidential scholar and Pulitzer prize-winning historian, Goodwin (OPPOSITE) grew up in Brooklyn with an intense passion for the Dodgers—as documented in her memoir *Wait Till Next Year*—but has since become a converted Red Sox fan. Celebrated author Andre Dubus—no stranger to the Red Sox himself—is known for his gripping personal short stories and essays through works including *The Last Worthless Evening*, *Broken Vessels*, and *Dancing After Hours*.

SUPERIOR COURT JUDGE MARIA Lopez (OPPOSITE) has been touted by Republican and Democratic politicos alike. A member of the court since 1993, she also teaches trial advocacy at Boston University Law School. Keeping a watchful eye over the politicians and government officials is the staff of *The Boston Globe*, under the leadership of editor Matt Storin (ABOVE).

Bosto

The MEN IN BLUE AND THEIR firefighting counterparts hold the safety of Boston's citizens in their hands.

A SOLID EDUCATION AND QUALITY of life for children in the Boston area have been chief concerns of Mayor Thomas Menino, a tireless advocate for the city's youth (OPPOSITE). Also contributing are Sister Jeanne Marie Gribaudo (LEFT), a youth advisor to the mayor, and T. Berry Brazelton (RIGHT), internationally known author, pediatrician, and child-rearing expert.

© CAMI JOHNSON

AH, THE GOOD LIFE: IN BEAN-
town, whatever your age or
species, it can be simply *spec*tacular.

© ADRIAN MILLER

S INCE THE FIRST RACE WAS WON in 1897 by John J. McDermott with a time of 2:55:10, the Boston Athletic Association Boston Marathon has remained at the pinnacle of the sport. From its starting line in the suburb of Hopkinton (OPPO-SITE) to the legendary Heartbreak Hill (LEFT)—where many runners wind up either dropping out or falling out—the world's oldest marathon has produced a wealth of champions, including Ethiopian runner Fatuma Roba, women's winner in 1997 and 1998 (RIGHT).

THE NEW ENGLAND PATRIOTS have become one of the NFL's most winning franchises in recent years, with stars like quarterback Drew Bledsoe (TOP RIGHT) leading them to Super Bowl XXXI in January 1997, where they fought—albeit without success—the Green Bay Packers.

Both horse racing and base-ball cast long shadows over the city. For a day at the races Boston-style, Suffolk Downs is the place. The state's first major horse racing track, the Downs has hosted such equine legends as Seabiscuit, Cigar, and Whirlaway since opening its gates in 1935. A champion in his own right, former pitching ace Roger Clemens broke the hearts of countless Boston fans in 1996 when he signed as a free agent with the Toronto Blue Jays after 13 seasons in a Red Sox uniform.

Bosto

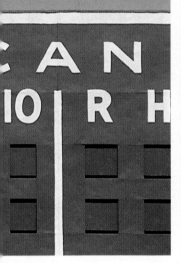

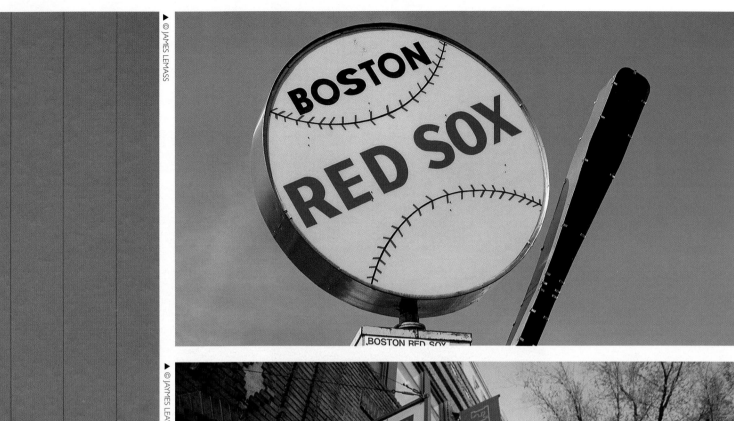

© JAYMES LEAVITT

F ROM ITS CLASSIC, HAND-
operated scoreboard to the
Green Monster wall in left field,
Fenway Park has been holy ground
to the Red Sox nation since it opened
in 1912. Sadly, it's one of just a few
old-time major-league ballparks still
around.

W HILE BOSTON GARDEN MAY have met the wrecking ball to make way for the new Fleet Center (BOTTOM), the round-ball legacy of the Celtics continues. From NBA Hall of Famer Larry Bird (TOP RIGHT) to hotshot new-comer Antoine Walker (OPPOSITE), the Celtics are a vastly popular component of Boston's professional sports scene.

Bosto

T HE UNDER-ACCLAIMED HEROES
of Boston transportation: the
people who build the highway tun-
nels and the hacks who drive the
cabs. Without them, the city would
likely screech to a halt.

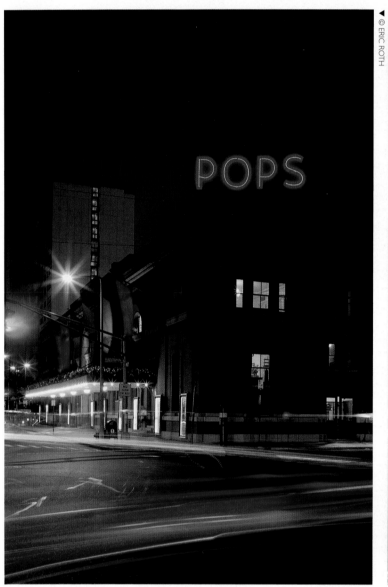

Bosto

A LONG THE CENTRAL ARTERY, Beantown after dark might include a stop at the regal Symphony Hall, home of the city's Boston Pops and Boston Symphony Orchestra (OPPOSITE LEFT). Along the water- front, the shimmering Custom House has the distinction of being the city's first skyscraper—built in the 1840s and expanded in 1913 with the addition of a majestic clock tower (OPPOSITE RIGHT).

Bostc

THE OMNIPRESENT CITGO sign—sometimes called The God of Kenmore Square—bathes the area in glowing light. Among Boston's busiest intersections, Kenmore is the home of countless nightclubs, as well as Fenway Park and Boston University.

B OSTON STREET MUSICIANS HELP
set the tempo of the city at
busy intersections and squares, and
underground at seemingly every stop
along the T—Boston's knot of
subway and streetcar lines.

W HEN SPRING FINALLY ARRIVES, Bostonians take once again to the streets and parks—for biking, skateboarding, or chatting over coffee (PAGE 150). Along the Charles River is the gorgeous Esplanade, a favorite spot for running, walking, or whiling away a beautiful sunny afternoon (PAGE 151).

Bosto

W HETHER YOUR PASSION IS
sculling or sailing, the Charles
River is an aquatic oasis. The geographic separator between Boston
and Cambridge, the Charles plays
host to numerous rowing teams, with
boathouses for two prep schools,
four colleges, and three boat clubs.
It's also a great place to take in the
sunrise (PAGES 154 AND 155).

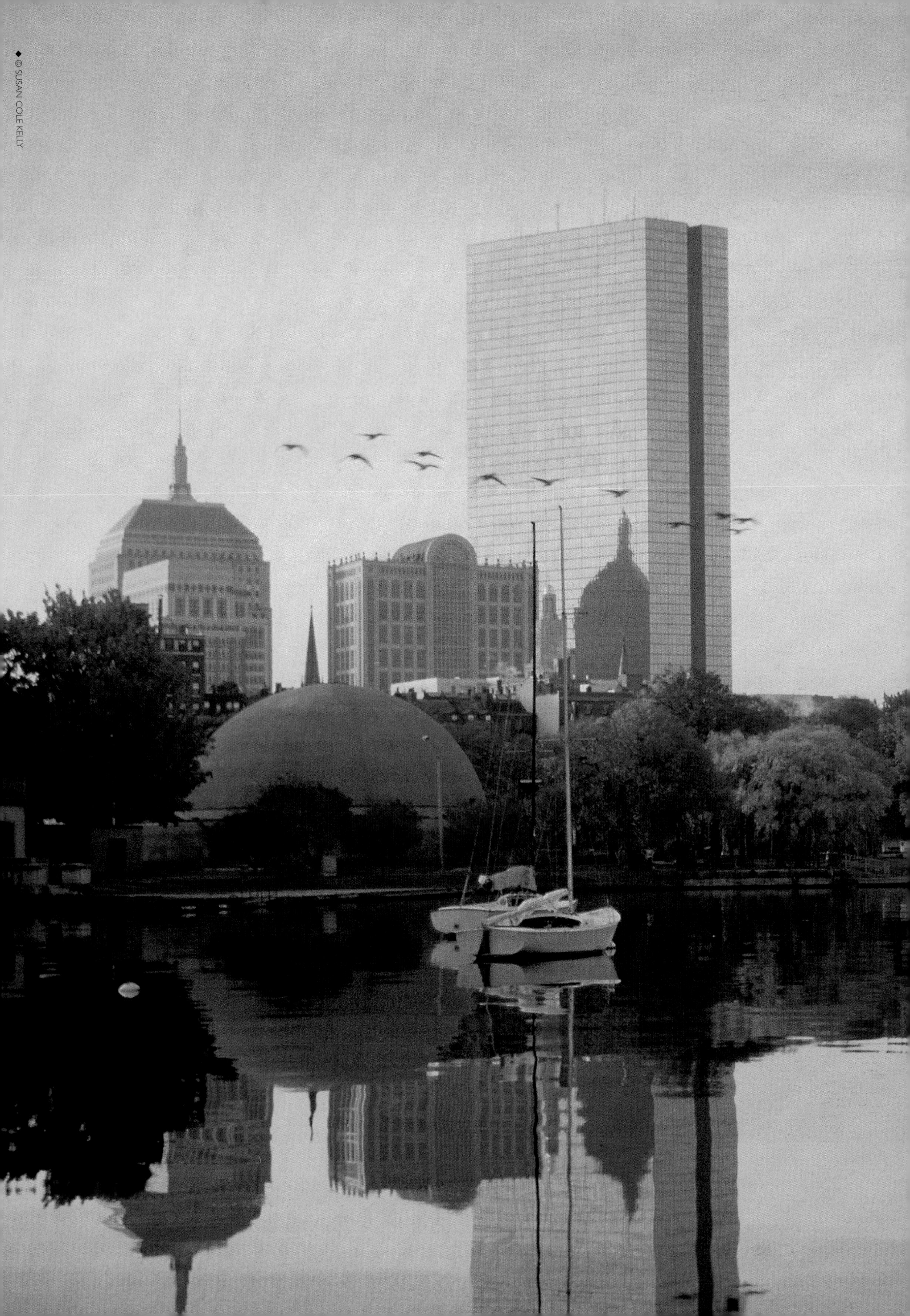

◆ © SUSAN COLE KELLY

Each July 4, more than 300,000 patriotic faithful show their colors at Hatch Shell on the Charles River. Festivities center around a concert by the Boston Pops Orchestra, featuring rousing music, such as *The William Tell Overture*, and a dazzling fireworks display to end the evening.

Bosto

B OSTON'S SMALL BUT VIBRANT Chinatown celebrates the Chinese New Year with pride, gusto, and liberal amounts of fireworks. An economic victim of 1960s sub- urban flight, the area has enjoyed a resurgence of late, with restaurants flourishing, grocery stores bustling, and countless shops and boutiques offering a plethora of Asian goods.

Bosto

Boston's First Night cele-
brations began in 1975 based
on an idea cooked up by Clara
Wainwright (ABOVE) and some of
her artist friends. The New Year's
Eve wingding features arts events at
more than 50 sites throughout the
city, including Copley Square, where
dramatic ice sculptures shimmer
among the holiday lights (OPPOSITE
LEFT). The Grand Procession artists'
parade down Boylston Street produces an explosion of glitz and
color of its own (OPPOSITE RIGHT).

Bosto

D RESS TO IMPRESS IF YOU MUST, but whatever may be falling, it's wise to mind the elements when at work or play.

Bosto

A DECIDEDLY PROGRESSIVE CITY, Boston is at the forefront of many a fashion frontier. Whether born in one of the area's salons, such as Solus (OPPOSITE), or imported for a new hair products show launched by acclaimed stylist-to-the-stars John Sahag (LEFT), the correct coiffure is the thing, dahling.

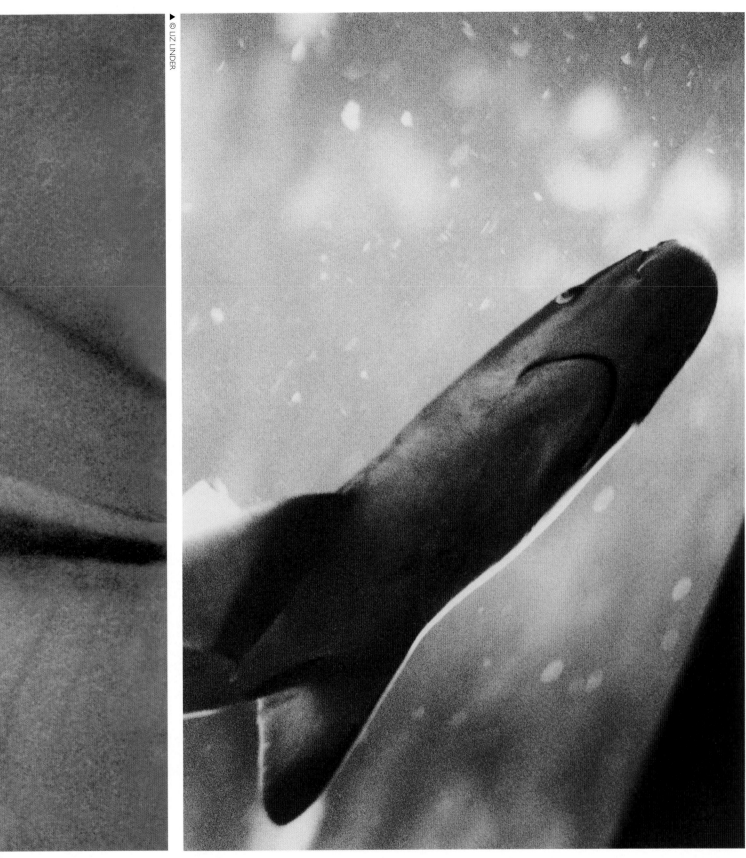

THE COUNTRY'S FIRST EXCLU-sively anthropological museum can be found, along with stuffed bats and other mounted critters, at Harvard University's Peabody Mu-seum of Archaeology and Ethnology, founded in 1866 (OPPOSITE). For a look at the area's aquatic life, become one of the 1.3 million annual visitors to the New England Aquarium (ABOVE). Opened in 1969, the facility recently added a new west wing and has an IMAX theater and east wing in the works.

Bosto

THE WATERS OF BOSTON AND Cambridge offer countless diversions, whether fishing for salmon or trout at the Emerald Necklace's Jamaica Pond or sculling on the Charles River.

Boston

AMID THE MASSIVE SPRAWL OF the 400-year-old Harvard Yard are some cozy spots to take in a book or bask in a moment of peaceful solitude, away from the bustle of the university and nearby Harvard Square.

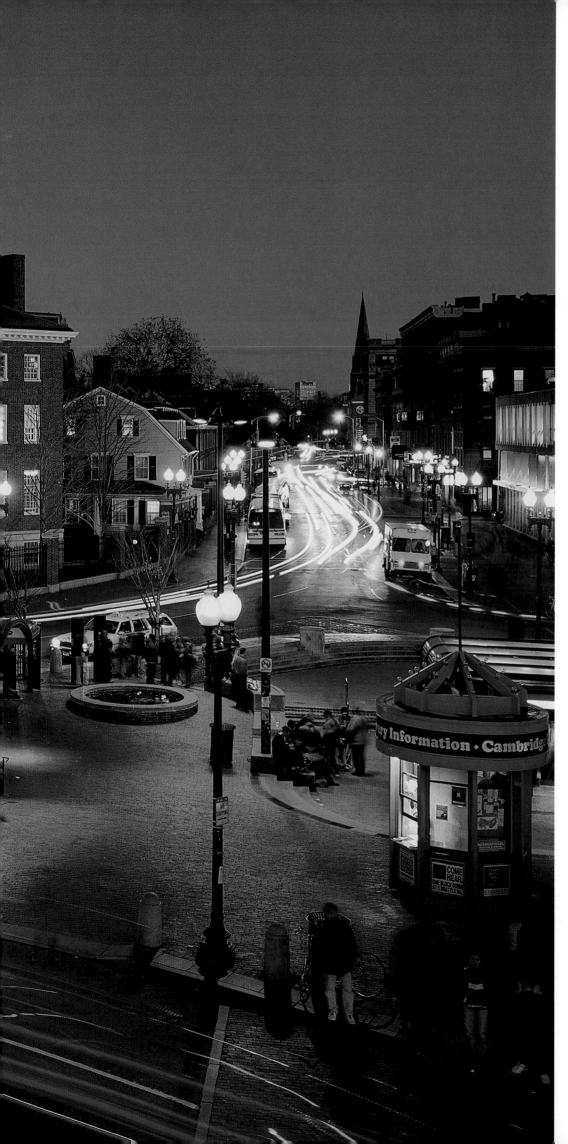

BOTH THE BIRTHPLACE AND the emotional center of Cambridge, Harvard Square, founded in 1630, remains the heart of this university town.

Tʜᴇ Oᴜᴛ ᴏꜰ Tᴏᴡɴ Nᴇᴡs is a focal point of Harvard Square—for its vast array of newspapers and magazines, and as a meeting place for locals and tourists alike (ᴏᴘᴘᴏsɪᴛᴇ). The square offers an intoxicating collection of characters, sidewalk brides, and storytellers, such as local yarnsman Brother Blue (ᴛᴏᴘ ʀɪɢʜᴛ).

Mitchel Resnick and Carl Malamud are among the fringe leaders on the technological front in metropolitan Boston. Resnick (OPPOSITE) is a Lego-obsessed author and computer wiz at the MIT Media Lab who has blazed new trails in child education. Malamud (TOP) is both an outspoken advocate of civil liberties and the president and founder of the Internet Multicasting Service research group. Each could be considered a Superman in his chosen field, having honed their skills at the internationally respected Massachusetts Institute of Technology (PAGES 186 AND 187).

Sᴍᴏᴋᴇ 'ᴇᴍ ɪꜰ ʏᴏᴜ ɢᴏᴛ 'ᴇᴍ: Although many area restaurants are now smoke-free, Boston and Cambridge have seen a boom in cigar stores and smoking lounges. Even the bronze likeness in Quincy Market of noted stogie puffer Red Auerbach is sporting a tobacco torpedo. The legendary coach of the Boston Celtics is reported to be the only person allowed to light up at the team's new Fleet Center.

REGARDLESS OF THE SOURCE of precipitation, fun times for all are available in Boston. The Back Bay's Public Garden offers cool relief from the summertime heat via its many fountains (OPPOSITE TOP), not to mention the arctic thrills and spills that come amid the snowfalls of winter (LEFT). And you can count on a downfall of confetti during the many festivals held in the Italian section of the North End (OPPOSITE BOTTOM).

Bosto

S EASONAL BEAUTY ABOUNDS
in the tranquility of a snow-
blanketed Commonwealth Avenue,
a sharp contrast to the typical hustle
and bustle of this Back Bay artery
(TOP). Along nearby Marlborough
Street (BOTTOM), 19th-century homes
bedecked in holiday decorations
display the quintessential charm of
the area, as does the French Library
(OPPOSITE BOTTOM), with its salon
designed in the style of Empress
Josephine's private parlor at
Malmaison.

Bosto

R ED PARKAS ABLAZE IN THE
pristine snow, members of the
City Year youth service project—the
model for President Clinton's national
youth service corps—warm up in
front of Copley Square's Trinity
Church (OPPOSITE). Across the river
in Cambridge, a walk through the
winterland of Harvard Square is the
order of the day (ABOVE).

BOSTONIANS LOVE TO SWIM, but few are as zealous as the L Street Brownies of South Boston (OPPOSITE TOP), a brave crew of human polar bears who take a ceremonial plunge every New Year's Day into icy Dorchester Bay.

F OR WATER REVELERS OF ALL ages, Revere Beach is an ideal place to beat the Boston heat. The first publicly owned beach in the United States, Revere draws summer weekend crowds of up to 100,000 during the peak months of July and August.

Bosto

H ISTORIC GAY HEAD LIGHT SITS
160 feet above the sea on the
western side of Martha's Vineyard.
Originally made of wood in 1799,
the current lighthouse tower was
built in 1856 of brick. The surrounding land today is owned by
the Wampanaog tribe, protectors
of the scenic spot's clay cliffs.

Bosto

BEAUTIFUL WALDEN POND has been immortalized in words by transcendentalist author Henry David Thoreau, who fled to the area for a two-year period to escape what he considered the in-dignity and hypocrisy of Concord city life. Thoreau's one-room cabin is no longer, but the site and sur-rounding pathways are protected and preserved today by the Walden Pond State Reservation.

Plimoth Plantation is a re-creation of a 17th-century Pilgrim settlement and a veritable history book come to life. Not only are the buildings and gardens repli-cated, but the day-to-day life of the country's early settlers is reenacted—from authentic dialect to period clothing.

O F THE MORE THAN 30 ISLANDS in the outer harbor, Thompson Island is one of the loveliest (PAGES 210-213). The privately owned spot—riddled with meadows and saltwater marshes—is the home base for an Outward Bound youth organization program.

T O APPRECIATE THE FULL CHARACTER OF BOSTON, ONE MU:
understand that, while the city is fervently proud of its histo
and traditions, it is always looking toward the future. State Stre
Corporation is a perfect embodiment of this thinking. Founded
1792, this local institution is a mainstay in Boston's Financial Distric
and a pacesetter in the ever changing arena of global financ

### Serving Institutional Investors

With $4.8 trillion in assets under custody and $504 billion in assets under management, State Street is a leading servicer and manager of financial assets worldwide. The nation's largest mutual fund custodian, with nearly 40 percent of the industry's funds under custody, State Street has been ranked the largest U.S. master trust custodian bank every year since 1986. It is also the largest global custodian in Australia and Canada, the largest manager of U.S. tax-exempt assets, the largest manager of international index assets, and the third-largest U.S. equity index manager.

State Street serves a broad cross section of customers: institutional investors and investment firms that buy and sell securities; corporations and government agencies that issue investment securities; and security brokers and dealers who manage mutual funds and mediate between buyers and sellers of stocks and bonds. State Street provides these institutional customers with an array of services and capabilities, including accounting, foreign exchange, cash management, record keeping, securities lending, performance and analytic measurement, daily pricing, and decision support tools.

More important, the institutional investor benefits from State Street's expansive view of the institutional investment landscape. State Street endeavors to gain a comple understanding of a client's operations and future goals in order to provide the client with the greates benefits of its financial and technical expertise.

While other companies talk of "listening to the voice of the customer," State Street's success speaks for itself. Since 1977, the corporation has enjoyed 21 consecu tive years of double-digit earnings per-share growth. In addition, State Street's compounded annual growth rate has been 17 percent or more over the last 16 years. With well-deserved pride in State Street

STATE STREET CORPORATION ENDEAVORS TO GAIN A COMPLETE UNDERSTANDING OF A CLIENT'S OPERATIONS AND FUTURE GOALS IN ORDER TO PROVIDE THE CLIENT WITH THE GREATEST BENEFITS OF ITS FINANCIAL AND TECHNICAL EXPERTISE.

S INCE 1904, THE GEORGE B.H. MACOMBER COMPANY HAS been renowned for bringing construction management expertise to corporate and institutional clients throughout New England. Still in the hands of the Macomber family, the company enters the 21st century prepared to meet the most demanding construction challenges with innovative, forward-thinking approaches.

### An Enlightened Company

Today's Macomber is an innovative construction management firm that caters to the needs of a select group of corporate clients, including Fidelity Investments, State Street Corporation, EMC Corporation, and Hewlett-Packard; medical clients, such as University of Massachusetts Memorial Health Care Systems, Beth Israel Hospital, and Joslin Diabetes Center; and educational institutions, such as Boston College, Dartmouth College, and Massachusetts Institute of Technology. Macomber distinguishes itself with an enlightened, team-based approach to construction management.

Every individual at Macomber—from field engineer to president—works as a full-service partner to the client. According to Macomber Vice President John Henderson, "It translates into an ability to anticipate and communicate problems, issues, and answers so that everyone who feeds into the process understands them. It's where mistakes are eliminated, costs are reduced, and time to execute the work is reduced. We're able to do all of that because the team has a more complete understanding of the dynamics of the project."

In the case of a renovation project, a Macomber team uses its combined skill set to go into a facility, do a comprehensive analysis, and then complete the project without shutting the facility down. "You have to be really efficient to do that," says Henderson, "and you need the expertise to be able to come in, and—as a team—plan it out and execute it. With the demands of today's jobs and the speed at which we are moving, no one individual can carry the weight by themselves."

### Speaking the Language

Macomber's clientele have one thing in common: They exist in a framework in which change is constant and has a direct effect on their facilities needs. Changes in the financial services industry demand people-intensive and systems-intensive solutions. This translates into a need for flexible use of space and lightning-quick response. Medical institutions are being challenged to respond to upheavals in every aspect of their services and operations—changes that, in many cases, exceed the normal cycle of planning and construction. Their need is for expertise concerning their future options and resource allocation. Educational institutions are in heated competition for high-caliber students and educators, and many are in a rush to build new facilities and to maximize the use of existing ones.

All of these organizations have found that process management in a complex, fast-paced environment requires a team-based approach. With Macomber as their construction partner, they have an integrated team that speaks their language and understands how their business needs and construction needs are linked.

Macomber's success ultimately boils down to three principles: communication, continuous improvement, and management principles based on human potential. According to Henderson, "Macomber is a learning organization that aspires to raise every single human being in the company to their highest potential both as an independent thinker and as an independent manager. It's a tremendous challenge in any business, and it's what we're dedicated to." Because of this dedication, Macomber is well positioned for a second century of service and excellence.

THE MIT BIOLOGY BUILDING, CONSTRUCTED BY GEORGE B.H. MACOMBER COMPANY, IS A STATE-OF-THE-ART RESEARCH AND TEACHING FACILITY IN CAMBRIDGE, MASSACHUSETTS (TOP).

EVERY INDIVIDUAL AT MACOMBER—FROM FIELD ENGINEER TO PRESIDENT—WORKS AS A FULL-SERVICE PARTNER TO THE CLIENT (BOTTOM).

# Boston University

Since 1869, Boston University has been an integral part of the intellectual, cultural, and social life of Boston. The third-largest independent university in the nation, Boston University has an international reputation for teaching, scholarship, and research. ❧ Today, Boston University has a student enrollment of nearly 30,000 and a faculty of more than

3,000, including three Nobel Prize winners and the nation's poet laureate. The university's 15 schools and colleges offer more than 250 graduate and undergraduate programs in the liberal arts, communication, the sciences, engineering, law, medicine, dentistry, management, the performing and visual arts, social work, and theology.

Boston University is proud of its commitment to be directly involved with the artistic, economic, social, intellectual, and educational life of the community and the world. The university is also committed to providing educational opportunity to all, regardless of gender, race, or creed.

In 1872, Boston University became the first university in the nation to open all its divisions to female students, and in 1877, Helen Magill became the first woman to receive a Ph.D. from an American university. From the beginning, the university has attracted African-American and other minority students, including Dr. Martin Luther King Jr., who received his doctorate from Boston University's Graduate School of Arts and Sciences in 1955. In recent years, the university has drawn more international students, and from more countries, than any other in the nation, with more than 4,500 graduate and undergraduate students from abroad.

More than 226,000 alumni live in 135 countries and all 50 U.S. states.

### Serving the Community

In the heart of the city, and in the service of the city"—These words were used 90 years ago by Lemuel Murlin, Boston University third president, to describe the university's relationship with the city of Boston, and are still a watch word for the university's present-day faculty and administration. Today, the university serves the community in many ways.

During 1997, Boston University, its students, and its visitors spent more than $1 billion in the com-

onwealth of Massachusetts, with
otal economic impact of nearly
.2 billion. More than 22,000 area
idents are employed by the univer-
y, and an estimated 17,000 jobs
re created indirectly via university
ending. The university purchased
o5 million in goods and services
m Massachusetts companies, and
ident economic activity added
ore than $236 million to the
a's economy.

Boston University has also been
major source of construction activ-
in the city, creating more than
o construction jobs and spending
ore than $75 million on construc-
n projects in 1996 alone. The
iversity's nine-story Center for
otonics Research, completed in
97, is a mecca for the study of
ht and its application to new tech-
logies. The building, built at a cost
$80 million, contains research
s, an incubator/prototyping
nter for emerging businesses,
d instructional facilities.

## Creating Innovative Partnerships

In 1989, Boston University and the neighboring city of Chelsea established an unprecedented, long-term partnership, with the university assuming the responsibility of managing and rebuilding the city's schools. The program has been hailed as a model for restoring excellence to urban school systems. Highlights of the project include strengthened academic standards, curriculum reform, professional development programs for teachers, and an early childhood program that provides Chelsea's preschoolers with instruction, good nutrition, and social and physical development programs. Currently, 80 percent of Chelsea's three- and four-year-olds receive some form of educational day care.

The Boston Medical Center is an innovative partnership that emphasizes community-based care. The nonprofit institution, created by the 1996 merger of the Boston University Medical Center Hospital, Boston City Hospital, and Boston Specialty and Rehabilitation Hospital, serves all patients, regardless of ability to pay.

One of every two uninsured patients in Boston seeking medical care finds it at the Boston Medical Center. The university runs numerous health care programs for the homeless and the elderly, offers free vaccinations and health screenings, and runs telephone hot lines to provide information and referral services.

## Contributing to a Better Future

As Boston University approaches the new millennium, the institution continues to redefine the role of the university in modern society. The Boston University of the 21st century will continue to honor the best of the academic tradition while developing innovative ways to serve the community.

CLOCKWISE FROM TOP LEFT:
THE 112-ACRE MAIN CAMPUS STRETCHES
FOR MORE THAN A MILE ALONG THE
BANKS OF THE CHARLES RIVER, FROM
THE CITY'S HISTORIC BACK BAY DISTRICT
TO THE ALLSTON NEIGHBORHOOD.

AS AN URBAN CAMPUS WITH A LARGE
CONTINGENT OF INTERNATIONAL STU-
DENTS, BOSTON UNIVERSITY OFFERS
ITS STUDENTS AN EXCEPTIONALLY
RICH CULTURAL AND INTELLECTUAL
ENVIRONMENT.

ATHLETICS IS AN IMPORTANT PART
OF STUDENT LIFE, AND BOSTON
UNIVERSITY'S NATIONALLY RANKED
HOCKEY TEAM BRINGS THE EXCITE-
MENT TO A FEVER PITCH AT THE AN-
NUAL BEANPOT TOURNAMENT AMONG
AREA COLLEGES.

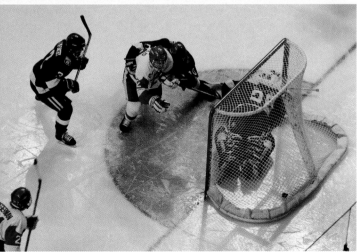

BOSTON UNIVERSITY PHOTO SERVICES

I N 1872, WHEN EBEN JORDAN AND FIVE OTHER LOCAL BUSINESSMEN decided to launch *The Boston Globe,* the city was already home to 10 newspapers competing for readers and advertisers. Convinced that Bostonians would respond to a superior commercial and business journal of outspoken independence, the group pooled $150,000, and on March 4 of that year, they produced the first

*Globe*—all eight pages of it.

The public, however, wasn't excited. Circulation remained low, and the Great Boston Fire of November 9, 1872—which gutted 65 acres downtown—prompted most of the newspaper's original investors to abandon the project due to financial hardship. As the sole remaining backer, Jordan turned to General Charles H. Taylor. A former Civil War soldier, stringer for the *New York Tribune,* and secretary to the governor of Massachusetts, Taylor signed on as temporary business manager in August 1873 and never left. Today, *The Boston Globe* is the region's dominant daily newspaper, with a circulation of nearly 500,000 daily and nearly 760,000 on Sunday.

Taylor, who transformed the *Globe* into a strong and respected voice, headed the *Globe* until 1921. Since then, management has continued in the hands of the Taylor family. William O. Taylor stepped into his father's shoes in 1921 and guided the paper until 1955, when he was succeeded by his son, William Davis Taylor. In 1978, General Taylor's great-grandson, William O. Taylor II, took over the office of publisher, a position he held until 1997, when his cousin, Benjamin B. Taylor, took the helm.

In 1973, *The Boston Globe* became a subsidiary of the newly formed Affiliated Publications, a publicly traded holding company owned primarily by members of the Taylor and Jordan families. In subsequent

the best way to preserve the character and mission of the *Globe*, the agreement included provisions for the *Globe* to maintain editorial control and remain a Massachusetts-based corporation, as well as to retain other business activities.

### Meeting the Changing Needs of Boston-Area Readers

Over the years, the *Globe* has been an innovative and sometimes controversial newspaper. It burst onto the national scene, for example, during the Vietnam War years, publishing the *Pentagon Papers* and becoming one of the first newspapers to call for an end to U.S. involvement in Southeast Asia. Its coverage of the desegregation of Boston Public Schools in the

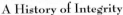

### A History of Integrity

Under Taylor's stewardship, the *Globe* was one of the first newspapers in the country to embrace impartial coverage of political issues. Taylor also expanded the publication's family-oriented coverage by adding material for women and children, and introduced a baseball column to attract young people. Five years after taking over, Taylor had turned the paper into the most innovative in the city, with a circulation of 50,000.

years, Affiliated expanded its reach with investments in television, radio, magazines, and cellular communications. By the early 1990s, the holding company had returned to its newspaper roots, divesting itself of most of the other properties at significant profit to shareholders.

The biggest change in ownership came in 1993, when Affiliated joined forces with The New York Times Company in the largest single newspaper merger and acquisition in U.S. history. Viewed as

early 1970s—which, at one point, led to shots being fired through the *Globe*'s windows—garnered a Pulitzer Prize for public service in 1975. In all, the newspaper has collected 15 Pulitzer Prizes for journalistic excellence, including awards in 1980 for investigative reporting on waste and mismanagement within the city's public transportation system and in 1984 for its series on African-American employees in the workplace.

The *Globe*'s innovative development continued over the years, even

information from more than 65 partners, including broadcast stations, magazines, and other sources.

As the *Globe* has grown, it has also become a philanthropic force in the area. The Boston Globe Foundation, for example, distributes $2 million annually to local nonprofit agencies, funding causes as diverse as arts education, help for abused children, and literacy. In 1986, the foundation gave $1 million to the Boston Public Library for branch reading programs and the renovation of its main building.

The newspaper's best-known philanthropic effort is Globe Santa. Since 1956, this seasonal program has raised money to buy Christmas gifts for needy children. Globe Santa has received more than $1 million annually from readers in recent years, allowing it to reach nearly 60,000 children every year.

Change is a regular event at the *Globe*, and the newspaper will continue to adapt to community and reader needs. As it has for more than a century, *The Boston Globe* will maintain its New England perspective, and will remain deeply involved in the community that shaped it.

THE ORIGINAL *Globe* BUILDING, PICTURED CIRCA 1907, WAS LOCATED ON NEWSPAPER ROW IN DOWNTOWN BOSTON (TOP).

THE *Globe*'S MAIN HEADQUARTERS TODAY IS IN THE DORCHESTER SECTION OF BOSTON. THE PAPER ALSO HAS A PRINTING PLANT IN BILLERICA, AND A PACKAGING AND ASSEMBLY PLANT FOR SUNDAY INSERTS IN WESTWOOD (BOTTOM).

ring difficult financial times. In 87, during a recession, the paper augurated *New Hampshire eekly*, the first of six regional nday sections that are still published today. These zoned editions ver local stories and serve specific ographic areas. Also during the cession, a time that put a squeeze advertising revenues throughout e newspaper industry, the *Globe* ablished music and movie sec- ns, redesigned its magazine, panded the book pages, and ded sections for younger readers.

In late 1994, the *Globe* estab- hed Boston Globe Electronic blishing (BGEP), a subsidiary dicated to on-line presentation news and information about all ects of New England. BGEP gan operations in 1995, and today responsible for Boston.com, one the most popular sites on the orld Wide Web, offering content m *The Boston Globe*, as well as

A CONCLAVE OF CRANES DOTTING BOSTON'S SKYLINE STAND A towering symbols of the city's economic prosperity in the la 1990s—a trend galvanized by the Big Dig highway constructic project, a booming real estate market, a skyrocketing mutu funds industry, and a large university system that helps fill loc hotel rooms and restaurants. From the city skyline to th

surrounding suburbs, one of the movers behind the largest and most visible real estate transactions has been Meredith & Grew Incorporated.

From the erection of Copley Plaza to the demolition of the Boston Garden, which stopped traffic as drivers paused to glimpse remnants of Celtics and Bruins glory, Meredith & Grew has played a significant role in representing the developers and businesses shaping today's city. While the firm has roots intertwined with Boston's heritage, the company has remained at the forefront in the real estate industry by expanding both the depth and breadth of the business through the successful launching of new services and the execution of complex real estate transactions.

A full-service real estate company, Meredith & Grew offers brokerage, finance, appraisal, property and asset management, advisory services, and market research for the commercial and industrial markets. The firm's business diversity has helped it weather the ups and downs of the real estate market, such as the recession that began in the late 1980s and the Great Depression in the 1930s.

MEREDITH & GREW'S CORPORATE HEADQUARTERS IS LOCATED IN THE LANDMARK BUILDING IN BOSTON'S FINANCIAL DISTRICT (TOP).

MEREDITH & GREW EMPLOYEES VOLUNTEER AT THE HENRY GREW SCHOOL IN THE HYDE PARK SECTION OF BOSTON (BOTTOM).

## More than a Century of Achievements

Meredith & Grew got its start when James Morris Meredith, a native of England, opened a small real estate brokerage office at 4 Exchange Place in Boston in 1875. In 1891, Meredith formed a partnership with Edward Wigglesworth Grew, who was just 21 years old and fresh out of Harvard. They established new headquarters at 15 Congress Street, and Grew's addition expanded the scope of the business to include property management and the management of real estate trusts. He also had extensive contacts in Boston's financial community.

In 1920, the firm moved to 40 Central Street, where it remained until the beginning of World War II, when it relocated to 60 Congress Street. At that time, the company remained heavily involved in residential real estate and had outlying offices in the suburbs.

During the Commonwealth's postwar period of industrial expansion, Meredith & Grew was at the center of activity, enlarging its staf substantially in order to handle demand. In a few years, Meredith & Grew's brokers developed a number of industrial complexes along Route 128.

At the end of the 1940s, Boston redevelopment began in earnest, and the company's emphasis begar to shift away from industrial devel opment and back to its roots of property management. In additior with redevelopment and construction booming, Meredith & Grew became involved in appraisal work Meredith & Grew also landed itsel squarely in the office space busines when it handled the bidding on a

rcel of land on High Street. This
:ation would eventually become
ston's first major downtown of-
e building in more than 30 years:
e 16-story Travelers Insurance
•mpany building.

Today, Meredith & Grew's 21
rtners continue to build upon
eir collective real estate experience.
.e firm—which celebrates its
th anniversary in 2000—employs
•re than 135 professionals and
pport staff, and recently opened a
inch office for its finance depart-
•nt in Greenwich, Connecticut.
ace 1987, Meredith & Grew's
•adquarters has been at 160
deral Street in the heart of the
nancial District. While New
gland is the company's primary
.rket, Meredith & Grew is a
.rtner in ONCOR International—
.vorldwide affiliation of leading
al estate firms—and today repre-
its clients' interests in more than
• markets worldwide.

## Firm with Distinction

Vith its impressive history,
Meredith & Grew has
rned its reputation as Boston's

real estate authority, says Thomas
J. Hynes Jr., current president of
the company. The company's
annual market seminar, which is
20 years in the running, is attended
by 700 members of the corporate
community who come to hear
Meredith & Grew's insight. "People
use it as a benchmark in their real
estate calendars," says Hynes. "It
separates us from the competition."

Also setting Meredith & Grew
apart is the company's devotion to
the community. The company's
partners sit on the boards of numerous nonprofit, educational, business, and professional institutions.
Most recently, the company has
partnered with the Henry Grew
School, an elementary school in
Hyde Park named for Henry Grew,
grandfather of cofounder Edward.
A letter from the school's principal
came across Hynes' desk, seeking
help to improve the learning environment. "It was easy to relate to
the school's dilemma," says Hynes.

A history of forming relationships such as this and others has
helped establish Meredith & Grew as
a trusted partner in the community.

A commitment to staying ahead of
the technology curve by investing
in hardware and software has helped
keep Meredith & Grew on the cutting edge of the real estate business.
And an ongoing effort to grow the
business, in terms of services offered
as well as markets covered, ensures
Meredith & Grew will be a vibrant
and busy company for many years
to come.

Progress can be measured by many factors, but no one would dispute that the harnessing of electricity in the late 19th century was a major step forward in human history that ushered in the technological revolution of the 20th century. From radio tubes to transistors to semiconductors, Sager has grown along with this revolution from a venerated local supplier of electrical components to a global supplier and innovator, helping the pioneers of today's technological industries reach new heights.

Sager Electronics was a regional company until 1996, when it opened 17 new locations in the central and western regions of the United States, with corporate headquarters in Hingham.

### A Proud History

Sager opened its doors in 1887 as a supplier of speaking tubes—precursors to the modern-day intercom—which were used in the brownstone apartments of 19th-century Boston. As radio and electric

From radio tubes to transistors to semiconductors, Sager has grown along with the technological revolution from a venerated local supplier of electrical components to a global supplier and innovator.

lights came to prominence, Sager became a leading area supplier of electrical components. At one point, Sager was the largest distributor of Lionel electric trains in the United States, and in the 1920s, Sager was the first to broadcast reenactments of Boston Bruins hockey games, in which announcers took reports off the Teletype and dramatized them in the Boston Garden press box.

Sager was a prominent supplier of electrical components throughout the first half of the 20th century. In the 1960s, the company successfully migrated into the new arena of electronic components, and in 1977, the company moved to its new location in the Boston suburb of Hingham. Today, Sager is one of the top 20 component distributors in the world—and is one of only three privately held electronic distributors in North America.

Sager was a regional company until 1996, when it opened 17 new locations in the central and western regions of the United States. In early 1996, the firm had approximately 300 employees, which grew to more than 500 by 1998. Its annual revenues have grown proportionally, passing the $100 million mark in 1993 and the $200 million mark in 1997, and are closing in on the $300 million mark in 1998. Sager is rapidly making the jump to becoming a global distributor by extending its services into the Asian, European, Mexican, and South American marketplaces. With additional plans to expand in other major markets, Sager is truly a global distributor, positioned to most effectively service customers and manufacturers.

### Distributing Confidence

In today's fast-moving world, Sager's customers in the computer, military, and telecommunications industries are setting the pace for everyone else. Sager is ultimately in the business of distributing confidence that customers will get the products and services they need when they need them, and at the lowest possible acquisition cost. Given their market niche and the very competitive nature of the business, Sager must continually adjust to changing market conditions

Eighty percent of Sager's business is with firms having revenues from $20 million to $250 million, and Sager offers these mid-tier companies a wide range of products, as well as inventory, billing, engineering, and logistics support. Sager's larger competitors don't offer this kind of partnering relationship, and its mid-tier customers would need four or five other companies to replace what they receive by dealing with Sager.

Always a company with a strong orientation toward service, Sager has also invested heavily on both the quality and technology fronts. Sager is an ISO 9002-certified company.

## Utilizing Technology

In the technology arena, Sager outpaces some of its larger competitors, reinvesting a large part of its profits into infrastructure and operations. Sager's distribution center utilizes state-of-the-art technologies such as conveyor systems, carousel systems, and static shelving, and all transactions are recorded via wireless radio-frequency bar code technology. This technology gives Sager an accuracy and efficiency rating that is the envy of the industry.

Not surprisingly, Sager is deeply involved in Web and new media technology. Sager's Web site is designed with electronic commerce in mind; a customer can visit the site, get product specifications, place orders, and check pricing, inventory, and order status in real

time, keeping the company open for business worldwide, 24 hours a day, seven days a week. Sager also produces a CD-ROM—now available on its Web site—that allows an engineer to search for a part having various criteria, and find schematics and product specifications.

Sager also utilizes technologies such as automatic inventory replenishment systems (AIRS), electronic data interchange (EDI), and just-in-time delivery to minimize overhead for both Sager and its customers. With AIRS, customers get the benefits of volume pricing and automatic reordering, while maintaining cash flow and avoiding overstock. With EDI, all back-end transactions—including purchase orders, order acknowledgments, and payments—are transmitted

electronically. With just-in-time technology, factors such as projected customer needs, locations, and travel routes are evaluated in order to guarantee that a given part will be on the shelf wherever, whenever, and however the customer wants it. Sager also offers quoting services and software for the contract manufacturing industry, consolidated billing services, and on-site communications and warehousing personnel.

Despite its explosive growth and state-of-the-art technology, some things at Sager haven't changed since its founding. The notion that product and service are inseparable is the common thread between the Sager that started in the 19th century and the Sager that is rapidly accelerating into the 21st.

SAGER INVESTS IN TECHNOLOGY TO PROVIDE CUSTOMERS WITH EXCEPTIONAL SERVICE.

SAGER'S DISTRIBUTION CENTER IS EQUIPPED WITH STATE-OF-THE-ART MATERIAL HANDLING SYSTEMS.

WO OVERRIDING PRINCIPLES UNDERLIE SIMPLEX TIME RECORDER Co.'s operations: "Protecting people, property, and peace of mind" and "helping businesses find better ways to work." Headquartered in Gardner, Simplex is a leading multinational provider of fire detection, security, building communications, and workforce solutions. From Logan Airport to the Fleet Center

to large corporate buildings like the Prudential Center, Simplex products are at work throughout Massachusetts and the world.

Founder Edward G. Watkins' 1888 invention of the first time clock for tracking employee hours proved to be an innovative solution that set the course for Simplex's development. Watkins designed the time clock while working for his father, Gardner A. Watkins, in the engineering department of Heywood Brothers Company in Gardner. In 1894, Edward invented a more advanced time clock, which he named the Simplex time recorder because it was easy to use. Simplex Time Recorder Co. was incorporated in 1902 at 26 Sanborn Street in Gardner, with Edward serving as president.

Edward soon opened a branch in Chicago, in order to ensure that Simplex would have an office close to its customers. In doing so, he set a precedent that would become a hallmark of Simplex. The company also broadened its customer base in 1916 with the acquisition of two companies: the W.H. Bundy Time Recorder Company and Syracuse Time Card, both of New York.

Curtis "Curt" Watkins, Edward's son, took over the Simplex presidency in 1942, and went on to make an acquisition in 1958 that would define the company for the future and diversify its product line. With the acquisition of IBM's Time Recorder Division, Simplex catapulted to the top of the U.S. market for time recorder/master time clocks. In addition, the purchase thrust Simplex into the fire alarm and multiplex systems market. Under Curt's leadership, Simplex also opened factories in West Germany, England, and Trinidad.

E.G. Watkins, the son of Curt Watkins, took the helm in 1967, and has guided the company toward new technology and development of software-based products that manage a building's fire alarm, security, and communications systems, and provide advanced electronic workforce information capabilities.

In 1997, E.G. Watkins made another strategic acquisition with the purchase of Information Marketing Businesses Inc. (IMB), a Cambridge-based company that pioneered the development of labor management systems for the retail industry, specializing in labor forecasting and scheduling software.

## Systems, Solutions, and Service

Today, Simplex operates with three main business units: Building Systems, Workforce Solutions, and an extensive service and support organization. Major markets for Simplex's products include the health care, education, technology, institutional, industrial, transportation, commercial, and contractor sectors.

In building systems, Simplex is a leading worldwide provider of fire detection and alarm systems. The company's Building Systems product line also includes security, access control, closed-circuit television (CCTV), and communications (digital telephone, intercom, and nurse call systems) solutions. Key products in this division are the Simplex 4120 Fire Detection Network, the NT 3400™ Security Management Information System, and the TrueCom® family of sound and communications solutions.

In Simplex's Workforce Solutions division, the company's leading product is WinSTAR®, the industry's first Microsoft Windows®-based time and attendance system.

What differentiates Simplex is its network of 170 branch offices around the globe. The branches

HEADQUARTERED IN GARDNER, SIMPLEX TIME RECORDER CO. IS A LEADING MULTINATIONAL PROVIDER OF FIRE DETECTION, SECURITY, BUILDING COMMUNICATIONS, AND WORKFORCE SOLUTIONS.

e staffed by Simplex employees
nd dedicated to servicing custom-
s with certified technicians and
ctory-direct support and parts.
mplex's fleet of service vans—seen
aveling on the roads throughout
e United States and Canada—
e symbols of the company's com-
itment to customer service. And
ustomer service is the bottom
ne at Simplex. Throughout its
story, Simplex has been guided
y that business principle—and by
ree generations of the Watkins
mily. It's proved to be a recipe
r success. As the 21st century
pproaches, Simplex has become
global enterprise with more than
000 employees worldwide; a new,
ate-of-the-art, 680,000-square-foot
anufacturing and research-and-
velopment facility in Westminster;
mpany-owned subsidiaries in
anada, Australia, the Far East,
urope, and Latin America; repre-
ntatives in 65 countries; and
0,000 customers. Through reces-
ons, depressions, and changing
chnology, Simplex has stayed
n a steady course by providing
ventive and innovative technol-
y, focusing on customer service,
d making some important and
rategic acquisitions.

## trong Local Roots

A privately held company,
Simplex is proud of its family
eritage and its association with the
entral Massachusetts region. Gen-
ations of families from the local
ea have worked for Simplex over
e years, and many have stayed
ith the company their whole career.
s a result of the company's rapid
owth over the last decade, Simplex
constructing the new Corporate
eadquarters and Operations Center
n its 300-acre campus in nearby
estminster.

The company is also proud of
s quality customer service and its
ng-standing tradition of deliver-
g value to customers throughout
e life cycle of their Simplex system.
n example of how the company
uccessfully meets the needs of
ustomers is Simplex's Toronto
anch office, which recently earned
prestigious Pinnacle Award for

outstanding customer service from
the Building Owners and Managers
Association (BOMA) of Greater
Toronto.

Looking ahead, Simplex is
committed to remaining a leader
in its market segments by staying
on the leading edge of technology,
continuing to provide superior
customer service, and expanding
its international markets. The company recently opened a subsidiary
office in Mexico. As it has throughout its history, Simplex will con-

tinue this expansion course through
a careful and deliberate process of
partnering with customers and
logically extending the business
where opportunities exist.

And how does Simplex continue
to know what's on the minds of its
customers? By listening; through
focus groups, interviews, industry
panels, and other outreach efforts;
and by building lasting partnerships
with its customers. At Simplex,
the voice of the customer is always
heard.

SIMPLEX HAS A NETWORK OF 170
BRANCH OFFICES AROUND THE GLOBE.
STAFFED BY SIMPLEX EMPLOYEES, THE
BRANCHES ARE DEDICATED TO SERVICING
CUSTOMERS WITH CERTIFIED TECHNI-
CIANS AND FACTORY-DIRECT SUPPORT
AND PARTS.

I N 1819, Augustus Siebe—an immigrant Austrian artillery officer—invented the world's first underwater diving suit in London. Ninety years later, Edgar and Bennet Bristol started up an industrial gauge business in Foxboro, Massachusetts. Few would have imagined that by the end of the 20th century, these men's dreams would merge as the world's leading enterprise automation company.

Located 25 miles south of Boston, the historic town of Foxboro is renowned as a world center of automation excellence. Two of the most prestigious names in automation reside here: The Foxboro Company and its parent division, Siebe Intelligent Automation. Together, these world leaders have brought global recognition to this small New England community. Today, Foxboro is a major focal point in the highly competitive arena of enterprise automation. The success of these Siebe Group companies has been accompanied by steady job growth, financial stability, and the ever increasing, multimillion-dollar payrolls that now help to fuel the region's economy. In total, Siebe Intelligent Automation, part of the British-based Siebe Group, boasts worldwide employment of more than 20,000 and revenues exceeding $3 billion annually.

## Automation: The Business of Controlling Variables

The field of automation is exceedingly diverse. It involves measuring all types of variables, establishing ideal conditions for them—called "set points"—and controlling these variables via devices such as computers and electronic controllers. These variables can range from the temperatures and humidities found in commercial buildings, to the pressures inside a plastic molding machine, to the thousands of flow and related measurements encountered in a typical petroleum refinery. The end result of automation is that an ideal condition, once established, can

be repeated indefinitely. For the world's consumers, this means that breakfast cereal will always taste the same; lights will always go on when someone presses the switch; an automobile will operate smoothly and consistently on a given octane rating; and medications, clothing, household supplies, and countless other commodities will always live up to their published specifications. Automation constantly touches people's lives.

## Foxboro: An Unparalleled Record of Technological Leadership

Early in 1908, a small group of entrepreneurs moved to the town of Foxboro and began manufacturing gauges and simple instruments. Officially named The Foxboro Company—also known simply as Foxboro—the firm's products gained rapid recognition for their exceptional quality and reliability. Foxboro quickly became a mecca for the automation industry's early application pioneers. Today, the company's highly respected automation experts can be found in every corner of the globe, working diligently to boost the operating performance of plants throughout the chemical, oil, paper, metals, food, and power process industries, as well as dozens of others.

In 1987, Foxboro introduced the first of a new generation of industrial automation systems, its Intelligent Automation (I/A) Series system. This was the world's first open industrial automation system based on universal industry standards. As a result, Foxboro's I/A Series was the first system that could easily accommodate newly emerging technologies and software, enabling it to remain perpetually state-of-the art. The I/A Series system's openness also became a key ingredient

PRECISION FLOW MEASUREMENT DEVICES FROM SIEBE INTELLIGENT AUTOMATION ARE INSTALLED IN AN INDUSTRIAL MANUFACTURING PLANT. THESE DEVICES MONITOR FLOW IN A PROCESSING LINE 24 HOURS A DAY, 365 DAYS A YEAR, AND CONTINUOUSLY SEND THE RESULTING DATA TO A CENTRAL CONTROL ROOM (TOP).

BOSTON TO BRISBANE: THIS FUTURISTIC CONTROL CENTER EPITOMIZES SIEBE INTELLIGENT AUTOMATION'S CORE BUSINESSES, THE AUTOMATION OF COMPLEX INDUSTRIAL PROCESSES. HERE, AT BRITISH PETROLEUM'S REFINERY IN BULWER ISLAND, AUSTRALIA, FOXBORO INSTRUMENTS AND SYSTEMS ARE USED WITH HARDWARE AND SOFTWARE FROM SEVERAL OTHER SIEBE DIVISIONS TO TOTALLY AUTOMATE PRODUCTION AT THE HUGE COMPLEX (BOTTOM).

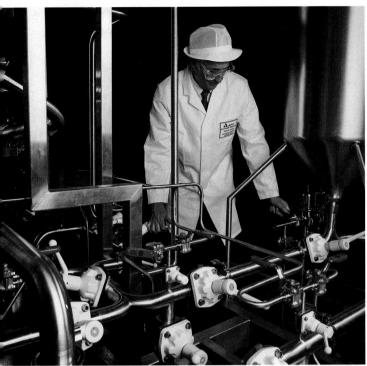

abling Siebe to incorporate newly acquired technologies into its expanding Intelligent Automation offering.

## Siebe Intelligent Automation: An Emerging Market Leader

Today, the Siebe Intelligent Automation division is a powerful combination of industry-leading brands and highly advanced technologies. Together, they offer customers the means to dramatically reduce the cost and improve the quality of their production and building systems. As a result, Siebe Intelligent Automation has emerged as the growth leader among top-tier names in enterprise automation.

Siebe consists of a number of world-class subsidiaries, including APV Company, one of the world's foremost suppliers of unit processing equipment and engineering services used for food-processing and pharmaceutical manufacturing industries. Barber-Colman is a leading supplier of specialized control instrumentation systems used in the plastics and thermal industries. Siebe produces advanced nuclear magnetic resonance devices to determine the on-line composition of industrial liquids and gases. Eurotherm is a leading U.K.-based supplier of temperature controls, variable-speed drives, and industrial recorders.

Other Siebe companies include Siebe Intelligent Building Systems, which creates leading-edge building automation and control systems, including a wide array of energy management software and equipment. Simulation Sciences is a leading global supplier of simulation software designed to optimize productivity and management decision making in the petroleum and chemical industries. Triconex is the leading supplier of safety shutdown systems for critical industrial processes. Triconex also supplies turbine controls, burner management systems, and fire- and gas-protection systems. Wonderware produces industry-leading MMI (man-machine interface)-based software and factory automation software suites.

In addition to The Foxboro Company, other divisions bearing the Foxboro name include Foxboro-Eckardt, one of Europe's leading suppliers of process automation and control systems. Foxboro Control Valves is a global supplier of process control valves and valve actuators. Foxboro SCADA—an acronym for sophisticated Supervisory Control and Data Acquisition—produces systems used in the power transmission as well as the oil and gas pipeline industries.

## Looking to the Future

Siebe Intelligent Automation has high expectations for an extremely bright future. Working together as a unified global organization, its member companies have harnessed their combined energies—products, technologies, and services—to ensure a total value to customers that is much greater than the sum of its parts. As it enters the 21st century, Siebe Intelligent Automation is fully committed to success through innovative technology, market leadership, and the lifetime satisfaction of its customers.

# The Stop & Shop Supermarket Company

T HE STOP & SHOP SUPERMARKET COMPANY HAS BEEN SERVING Bostonians and fellow New Englanders for more than 80 years. As customers have changed, so have the stores. ❧ In 1914, the Rabinovitz family established the Economy Grocery Stores Company in Somerville, Massachusetts. At the time, shopping for the family meant making trips to several specialty stores:

the butcher for meat, the baker for bread, and the produce market for fruits and vegetables. Thanks to the vision of family member Sidney Rabb, who joined the company in 1918, all this changed.

Rabb—affectionately known as Mr. Sidney—pioneered the idea of a large, self-service market in which individual sections would offer the products and services of specialty stores. This would provide customers convenience and lower prices, while allowing the store to take advantage of economies of scale. In 1935, the company opened the first full-service, modern supermarket in Cambridge, Massachusetts. Although the depression was still ravaging the area and the nation, Rabb's concept proved to be a huge success. He immediately embarked on a strategy of phasing out Economy's smaller grocery stores and focusing on supermarkets. By 1946, when the company changed its name to Stop & Shop, annual sales had risen to more than $42.5 million.

TOP: DURING THE HOLIDAYS, THE STOP & SHOP'S TURKEY EXPRESS PROVIDES TRUCKLOADS OF FOOD FOR NEEDY FAMILIES. PICTURED HERE ARE (FROM LEFT) BILL HOLMES, VICE PRESIDENT, STOP & SHOP; ADAM VINATIERI, NEW ENGLAND PATRIOT; AND CATHERINE D'AMATO, PRESIDENT, GREATER BOSTON FOOD BANK.

BOTTOM: STOP & SHOP PRIDES ITSELF ON BEING A COMPANY WITH A CON-SCIENCE—ONE IN WHICH GOOD CITIZEN-SHIP AND GOOD BUSINESS PRACTICES GO HAND IN HAND. PICTURED HERE IS PRESIDENT AND CEO WILLIAM J. GRIZE WITH CHILDREN FROM THE THOMAS GARDNER SCHOOL AT A NEW STORE OPENING IN ALLSTON.

The advent of suburban life and the prosperity that followed World War II led to constant and rapid growth for the chain. By 1959, sales had reached $200 million, and in 1970, topped $750 million. By 1985—when Rabb died after 60 years at the helm—sales had reached $1.8 billion. Presently, Stop & Shop is a $6 billion corporation, with 40,000 employees and nearly 200 stores.

## An Ongoing Commitment

R abb was not only a man of vision, but a man of principle; the principles that help Stop & Shop succeed today are the very same ones upon which the business was built. First and foremost, Stop & Shop always has paid attention to the voice of the customer not only by providing shoppers with selection, value, and quality, but also by going the extra mile to meet customer needs and concerns. In 1982, Stop & Shop pioneered the first superstore in New England. Today, more than 80 percent of the stores are Super Stop & Shops. With more than 20 shops under one roof and more than 52,000 items from which to choose, one-stop shopping is the company's hallmark.

Secondly, Stop & Shop is committed to treating customers and associates with respect, decency, and fairness: a commitment that includes making a difference in the community. Finally, Stop & Shop is dedicated to investing in the growth and development of its associates, encouraging innovation, and rewarding employees when they find new and better ways to do their jobs. As a result, Stop &

hop has maintained its position s an industry innovator.

## Giving Back to the Community

Stop & Shop prides itself on being a company with a conscience—one in which good citizenship and good business practices go hand in hand. The company backs this commitment by supporting more than 2,000 local nonprofit organizations, including the Jimmy Fund, Second Harvest National Food Bank Network, Juvenile Diabetes Foundation, Nature Conservancy, and United Way.

As a food retailer, Stop & Shop contributes more than $12 million per year to the fight against hunger. In addition to cash and product, associates give generously of their time and expertise. Through the Food for Friends program, individual stores adopt a local food pantry or soup kitchen and support with fund-raisers and food drives. During the holidays, the Turkey Express provides truckloads of food for needy families. Catherine D'Amato, president of the Greater Boston Food Bank, hails Stop & Shop as "a true champion in the fight against hunger."

Stop & Shop is especially proud of the leadership role it has taken in the fight against childhood cancer. Since 1991, the in-store Triple Winner Program has raised

more than $9 million to support the Jimmy Fund, a charity made popular by Boston sports icon Ted Williams. These contributions provide research and treatment in hopes that a cure for cancer eventually will be found, and help fund the Stop & Shop Family Pediatric Brain Tumor Clinic.

Stop & Shop also supports educational initiatives such as the company's partnership with local community colleges, which provides an opportunity for students to obtain hands-on business experience that will strengthen their skills

and open new doors for them after graduation.

The sentiments of millions of loyal Stop & Shop customers are best summed up by a homemaker who noted, "With my hectic schedule, Stop & Shop is where I go to save time. Its selection of products and full-service specialty departments means I only have to make one stop, leaving me more time to spend with my family." This is exactly what Rabb had in mind, and he would be proud of today's Stop & Shop— not only for what has changed, but also for what has stayed the same.

F ROM THE MICROWAVE OVEN TO THE WORLD'S FIRST ELECTRONIC depth sounder to the Patriot missile, Raytheon Company has made significant scientific and technological contributions to the quality and safety of our lives. A leader in developing defense technologies and in converting them for use in commercial markets, Raytheon has also played an important role in the economy of Massachusetts throughout its more than 75-year history.

Headquartered in Lexington, Massachusetts, Raytheon today is a $20 billion global technology leader operating in three core business segments: defense and commercial electronics, engineering and construction, and business and special mission aircraft. With more than 100,000 employees worldwide, Raytheon is one of the largest industrial corporations in the United States. Its extensive U.S. and international operations serve customers in more than 80 countries throughout the world.

## Rooted in Cambridge

R aytheon was founded in Cambridge in 1922 as the American Appliance Company. Building upon the company's early success in the field of radio tubes, company officials adopted the Raytheon name in 1925.

The company went on to play a key role in World War II through its technological innovations. Raytheon was the leading producer of radar tubes and complete radar systems during the war, providing the most important military advantage for Britain and the Allied Forces. An important Raytheon development was the microwave SG radar, a shipboard radar that was far superior to those carried in planes because German submarines could not tune in on their frequencies as they could with aircraft radar. In 1942, Raytheon began manufacturing the radar for PT boats, a feat other manufacturers previously had claimed was impossible, and by the end of the war, every U.S. PT boat was equipped with the Raytheon radar. Following the war, the firm became a pioneer in the field of missile guidance. In 1948, Raytheon became the first company to develop a missile guidance system that could hit a flying target.

In 1964, the company embarked on a major diversification program to broaden its business base by adding commercial operations. By the end of the decade, Raytheon had increased its commercial business to 45 percent of overall sales.

## Defense Technology in the Kitchen

R aytheon was the first to apply microwave energy to cooking with the invention of the microwave oven. It was Raytheon's 1965 acquisition of Amana Refrigeration, Inc.—an Iowa-based manufacturer of refrigerators and air conditioners— that ultimately made the microwave oven a fixture in U.S. households. In 1967, Raytheon introduced the Radarange™, the first countertop, domestic, 100-volt microwave oven, which retailed for just under $500.

The company continued to grow and evolve in the ensuing decades, but in 1991, Raytheon captured the world's attention. The Persian Gulf War put Raytheon's Patriot missile system to the test in a real military conflict when upgraded Patriot Advanced Capability Phase 2 (PAC-2) missiles successfully intercepted and destroyed

CLOCKWISE FROM TOP:
FROM REFINERIES—SUCH AS THIS ONE DESIGNED AND BUILT BY RAYTHEON— TO POWER PLANTS AND LIGHT RAIL LINES, RAYTHEON PROVIDES FULL- SERVICE, TURNKEY ENGINEERING AND CONSTRUCTION CAPABILITIES TO DIVERSE MARKETS AROUND THE WORLD.

RAYTHEON COMPANY IS A WORLD LEADER IN DESIGNING AND BUILDING AIR TRAFFIC CONTROL (ATC) SYSTEMS.

RAYTHEON'S PATRIOT IS THE WORLD'S MOST ADVANCED AIR DEFENSE SYSTEM, CAPABLE OF DEFENDING AGAINST THE ENTIRE SPECTRUM OF AIR DEFENSE THREATS. HERE, PATRIOT ANTENNAS UNDERGO TESTS DURING ADVERSE WEATHER CONDITIONS.

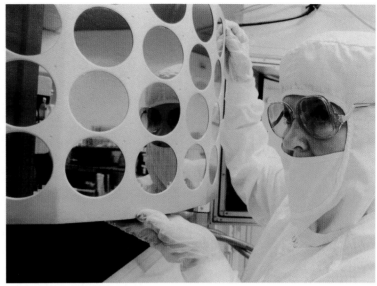

aqi Scud missiles fired at Israel ld Saudi Arabia. Credited with ving lives and changing the course f the war, the Patriot earned worldide recognition as the first missile l history to successfully engage a ostile ballistic missile in combat.

In 1997, Raytheon completed a ).5 billion merger with the defense perations of Hughes Electronics, a ading supplier of advanced defense ectronics systems and services. rom that merger—the largest transtion in Raytheon's history—came e creation of Raytheon Systems ompany, its consolidated defense usiness, which builds upon the ombined forces of the former aytheon Electronic Systems, aytheon E-Systems, Hughes, nd Texas Instruments' defense perations. Raytheon Systems ompany is now one of the largest efense contractors in the world, nd the third-largest U.S. military ontractor.

### ducation, Community, nd the Environment

aytheon's commitment to quality, ethical standards, and amwork extends to the company's ommunity involvement. Recognizing the complexity of today's ocial, educational, and environ-ental problems, Raytheon believes

it is important to be involved in various facets of the community to find long-term solutions. In the communities where its facilities are located, Raytheon's contributions program focuses on the strategic priorities of science, math, and technology education, with an emphasis on K-12 teacher professional development, student academic achievement, and postsecondary engineering education. For example, Raytheon is a major corporate sponsor of the Academic Decathlon, Math League, and science fair competitions for Massachusetts high school students.

The company is a leading supporter of engineering education at Northeastern University and University of Massachusetts. Raytheon is also a founding sponsor of MassPEP, the pre-engineering program designed to encourage Boston-area minority and female students to pursue careers in science and math. The company was honored in 1998 with the National Trustees Award from the Citizens' Scholarship Foundation of America.

Raytheon has also sponsored the Cultural Access Directory Web site, developed by Very Special Arts Massachusetts to promote accessibility of cultural facilities to people with disabilities. The company

was also an underwriter of the ScholarShop component of the Boston YMCA Black Achievers' College Path program.

Environmental issues are an ongoing concern for the company, which has been a leader in the Massachusetts Watershed Initiative and was a founding sponsor of WasteCap programs to promote recycling in Massachusetts. Raytheon received the 1997 Corporate Leadership Award from the Massachusetts Watershed Coalition.

Already a long-valued corporate citizen in Massachusetts and beyond, Raytheon, as always, is looking toward the future. The company plans to become an even more global company, remain a leader in defense and government electronics, continue growing its commercial business in both sales and profitability, and continue expanding defense technology into new commercial markets.

CLOCKWISE FROM TOP LEFT: RAYTHEON'S AIRCRAFT ARE DISTINGUISHED BY SUPERIOR WORKMANSHIP, ADVANCED TECHNOLOGY, AND LARGER, MORE COMMODIOUS CABINS, SUCH AS THOSE FOUND IN THE BEECHJET 400A LIGHT JET.

ORIGINALLY DEVELOPED FOR DEFENSE APPLICATIONS, RAYTHEON'S GALLIUM ARSENIDE MONOLITHIC MICROWAVE INTEGRATED CIRCUIT WAFER TECHNOLOGY IS HELPING TO ADVANCE THE ART OF WIRELESS COMMUNICATIONS.

RAYTHEON VOLUNTEERS VISIT CLASSROOMS TO HELP STUDENTS BETTER UNDERSTAND INDUSTRY'S IMPACT ON THE ENVIRONMENT.

D<small>R. F</small>RANK H. L<small>AHEY WAS ALREADY A PROMINENT</small> B<small>OSTON SURGEO</small> in 1923, when he gave up his positions on the Harvard and Tuf medical school faculties to concentrate on patient care in the newl established Lahey Clinic. In addition to his outstanding reputatio and ability to find talented, committed people, Lahey had a visior At the time, most physicians worked individually, and referre

difficult cases to teaching hospitals or outside specialists. Lahey foresaw a group practice where a number of physicians in varying specialties would work together as a team.

Since its start as a four-doctor practice, Lahey Clinic has become world renowned for its innovative approach to care, its patient-oriented environment, and its reputation as a place where some of the best specialists in their fields go for the

opportunity to practice intensive and complex medicine. Having recently celebrated its 75th year, Lahey Clinic is still driven by Lahey's vision.

### The Lahey Difference

L ahey Clinic Medical Center in Burlington, Massachusetts, encompasses an ambulatory care center and a 249-bed hospital. The medical center's staff of 250 doctors

and 3,000 support personnel provide care to more than 2,400 patients a day in virtually every specialty of medicine, from primary care to cardiac surgery. The center i a teaching hospital for Tufts University School of Medicine, maintaining residency and fellowship programs for more than 100 new physicians in 19 specialties. Lahey Clinic research programs include more than 200 clinical trial protocols, as well as participation in numerous national clinical trials.

A regional medical center in Peabody, Lahey Clinic Northshore provides primary and specialty care services to communities north of Boston, and Lahey's Symmes Hospital in Arlington provides Lahey outpatient care and other services. In addition, the Lahey Clinic network consists of more than 200 community-based doctor with sites in 37 Massachusetts towns Providing top-quality primary care services in their home communities, the physicians utilize local health care resources while maintaining access to the Lahey medica centers when complex specialty care is needed.

Lahey differs from most medica institutions in that physicians serve as full-time members of the staff, working in a centralized team environment that encourages consultation and referral. Lahey physicians are subject to a rigorous selection and training process. As part of the hiring process, for example, surgica candidates are observed by a Lahey staff member in the operating room and 98 percent of Lahey surgeons are either board certified or eligible for board certification.

Lahey's integrated approach to health care is welcomed by both doctors and patients. For physicians on Lahey's staff, it means the opportunity to concentrate

L<small>AHEY</small> C<small>LINIC</small> M<small>EDICAL</small> C<small>ENTER</small> <small>IS LOCATED IN</small> B<small>URLINGTON</small>, M<small>ASSACHUSETTS</small> (<small>TOP</small>).

P<small>HYSICIANS WORKING AS A TEAM IS A</small> <small>CORNERSTONE OF</small> L<small>AHEY'S PRACTICE</small> <small>OF MEDICINE</small> (<small>BOTTOM</small>).

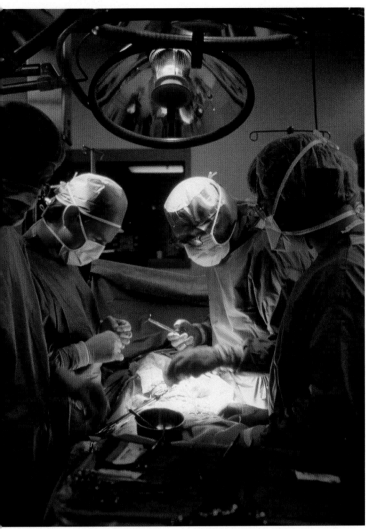

kidney and other urologic cancers. The clinic's cancer services include coordinated medical, surgical, and radiation therapy capabilities. Lahey operates the only high-dose radio-active-seed-implant program for prostate cancer in the northeastern United States, placing therapeutic radiation directly at the tumor site, thereby minimizing unwanted effects on normal tissue.

Lahey's Neurovascular Institute brings together neurologists, neuro-surgeons, radiologists, and other specialists to treat strokes and brain aneurysms with surgical and mini-mally invasive nonsurgical proce-dures. The center's Urology Institute encompasses the full spectrum of urologic services, including restora-tion of kidney function; laser therapy to treat superficial bladder cancer; upper- and lower-tract urinary re-construction; and treatment of benign prostate enlargement and prostate cancer, kidney cancer, and infertility.

The health care industry has seen tumultuous changes in the late 1990s and, in many ways, is merely catching up to Frank Lahey's vision of efficient, team-based, patient-oriented health care. Whatever the ailment, the Lahey patient is assured of access to world-class spe-cialists for diagnosis and treatment. The vision and commitment that were at the core of the first clinic live on in each member of the Lahey team today.

1 their areas of special interest hile maintaining close contact ith specialists in other disciplines. or patients at the major medical nters, it means centralized access the clinic's services through a ngle office for appointments, nsolidated medical records, and centralized billing system. Ulti-ately, Lahey Clinic places a vast etwork of medical, technological, d human resources at the service each patient.

## he Commitment Excellence

With its combination of advanced technology, skilled hysicians, and patient-oriented re, it's no surprise that Lahey linic is synonymous with leader-nip in a wide range of medical isciplines—and that patients me from around the world to ail themselves of its services.

Among Lahey Clinic's many nters of excellence, several are

worthy of note. Lahey's Breast Center services include risk assess-ment, diagnosis of breast cancer, and coordinated therapy, while the Breast Cancer Treatment Center brings surgeons, medical oncologists, and radiation oncologists together for timely evaluation and recom-mendation of treatment options for breast cancer patients.

Lahey's cardiovascular services include a full range of diagnostic, interventional, and surgical treat-ments of heart problems, including one of the largest cardiac surgery programs in the Boston area, with outcomes among the best in New England. Among program accom-plishments is Dr. Lars Svensson's performance of the first successful replacement of an entire aorta in one stage in 1993.

Lahey's cancer specialists offer treatment from a broad range of medical disciplines, including breast, ovarian, brain, lung, blad-der, and colon cancers, as well as

LAHEY'S SURGICAL CAPABILITIES ARE RENOWNED (TOP).

PHYSICIAN SKILL AND ADVANCED TECHNOLOGY ARE KEY TO LAHEY'S TOP-QUALITY CARE (BOTTOM).

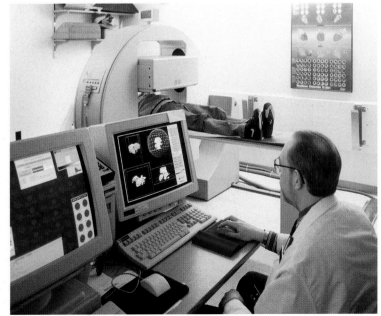

ESTLED AMID THE NEATLY LAID ROWS OF STREETS I Boston's historic Back Bay, against the architectural dichotom of the modern John Hancock Tower and the 122-year-ol Trinity Church, stands 500 Boylston Street, the present hom of MFS Investment Management®. For 75 years, MFS ha helped millions of investors realize their financial goal

In the process, it has also contributed to Boston's reputation as one of the world's premier financial centers.

It was MFS that gave birth in March 1924 to Massachusetts Investors Trust (MIT), America's first mutual fund and the first product in what has become a $5 trillion industry. This event has earned the firm a significant place in the financial history of the United States.

### Changing the Way America Invests

MIT accomplished for the world of investing what the telephone and the public subway, both invented in Boston, did for communication and transportation. In 1924, investing in individual stocks was an expensive proposition generally pursued by the wealthy. By allowing investors to purchase and redeem shares of a carefully managed portfolio of stocks with a minimal initial investment, MIT opened up to the general public

the world of professional money management.

Before MIT, only closed-end funds existed. Closed-end funds had a fixed capitalization, and supply and demand determined the price of the shares. MIT, in sharp contrast, would continuously issue new shares and redeem existing shares on demand. Investors liked this open-end concept because it offered them unlimited access to their money. This idea, pioneered by L. Sherman Adams and original MIT cotrustees Charles Learoyd and Ashton L. Carr, was greeted at first with skepticism. But when the investment community saw how well MIT weathered the stock market crash of 1929, the number of open-end mutual funds increased dramatically.

Seeded with a modest investment of $50,000, MIT has grown to more than $9.1 billion in assets under management. That initial $50,000 in paid-in capital was spread among 45 companies, including

General Electric and Eastman Kodak. Several stocks in that original portfolio still remain in the fund. Today MIT is the flagship fund of a flourishing financial services company that manages more than $87 billio for 3.3 million individual and institutional investors worldwide, as of June 30, 1998. All portfolios are actively managed, and holdings are subject to change.

Playing a significant role in the early success of MIT was Merrill Griswold, a young Boston lawyer who became the fund's fourth truste in 1925. Griswold was named the fund's chairman in 1932, a position he held until his retirement in 1953 In between, he was the single most influential force at MIT as well as in the mutual fund industry.

Pivoting off the success of MIT the trustees assumed management of another fund—Massachusetts Investors Second Fund (now Massachusetts Investors Growth Stock Fund)—in the early 1930s. By 1969 the year the trustees formed an investment management organization called Massachusetts Financial Services (MFS) to oversee the portfolios there were six funds. Thirty years later, MFS Investment Management offers dozens of additional investment

·oducts through financial advisers, ·cluding more than 50 mutual ·nds and an array of annuity, 401(k), ·d international products cover- ·g the entire investment spectrum. ·he firm—a subsidiary of Sun Life ·ssurance Company of Canada ·J.S.)—has also expanded its geo- ·aphical reach, with satellite offices · London, Sydney, Bahrain, and ·okyo.

### ·oston Is Home

While foreign offices have been established to accom- ·odate the firm's growing presence · overseas markets, Boston is still ·ry much MFS' home base. Each ·y, more than 1,900 employees ·ntribute their considerable tal- ·ts to MFS' products and services. ·hey include professionals who specialize in customer service, sales and marketing, technology, law, research, and money management, among other areas of expertise.

In addition to being a bona fide leader in the mutual fund industry, MFS has also demonstrated leadership in support of local causes. Over the past decade, MFS and its employees have donated nearly $1.5 million to the United Way of Massachusetts Bay. MFS also directly supports a number of medical and philanthropic organizations such as Children's Hospital, New England Medical Center, and the Boys and Girls Clubs of Boston. A percentage of the proceeds from the annual MFS Pro Championships, the country's oldest professional tennis tournament, is also earmarked for these causes.

Additionally, there has been a strong MFS presence at the City Year Serve-A-Thon, a citywide cleanup/beautification event held each fall. City Year is a national, nonprofit organization based in Boston that unites college-age people from diverse backgrounds for a year of full-time community service. As a result of employee interest and because of a strong belief in what City Year is doing for local youth, MFS became the corporate sponsor of the Serve-A-Thon in 1998.

MFS Investment Management has come a long way from its days as a conservative investment house run by three trustees. Today, it is a modern, progressive company with something to offer all types of investors. While the firm retains ties to its past via its logo (which proudly proclaims "We invented the mutual fund®") and its prudent investment philosophy, it is currently focusing more than ever on the future. A shining example is a program called MFS® Heritage Planning℠, which reaches out to MFS' millions of shareholders and their advisers to offer them assistance with the growing number of intergenerational financial-planning issues families face today. The program, launched in 1996, represents MFS' ongoing commitment to its investors—to help them plan not only their own futures, but also their children's and parents' futures. As it makes its way toward the century mark, MFS is poised to help the next generation of investors achieve its goals.

PORTFOLIO MANAGERS FOR THE MFS FAMILY OF MORE THAN 50 EQUITY AND FIXED-INCOME FUNDS EXECUTE BILLIONS OF DOLLARS IN PORTFOLIO PURCHASES AND SALES ANNUALLY (TOP LEFT).

PICTURED HERE IS A LIST OF MASSACHUSETTS INVESTORS TRUST'S HOLDINGS IN JULY 1924. THREE-QUARTERS OF A CENTURY LATER, THE FUND CONTINUES TO BE ACTIVELY MANAGED, ADHERING TO THE BASIC PHILOSOPHY OF INVESTING IN ESTABLISHED, WELL-MANAGED COMPANIES (TOP RIGHT).

FROM ITS MODEST BEGINNINGS AS A FIRM WITH ONE FUND RUN BY THREE TRUSTEES IN 1924, MFS INVESTMENT MANAGEMENT TODAY EMPLOYS MORE THAN 1,900 PEOPLE (BOTTOM LEFT AND RIGHT).

SECURITIES OWNED BY THE
**MASSACHUSETTS INVESTORS TRUST**
AS OF JULY 15, 1924

BANK AND INSURANCE

| Shares | Company | Cost |
|---|---|---|
| 3 | Boston Insurance Company | 682¼ |
| 5 | Springfield Fire & Marine Ins. Co. | 325 |
| | INDUSTRIAL AND MISCELLANEOUS | |
| 10 | American Radiator Co. | 102⅛ |
| 5 | American Tobacco Co. | 145¼ |
| 10 | Bates Manufacturing Co. | 200 |
| 10 | Eastman Kodak Co. of N.J. | 107⅝ |
| 5 | Farr Alpaca Co. | 172¾ |
| 5 | General Electric Co. | 232¼ |
| 50 | General Motors Co. | 13¼ |
| 10 | Island Creek Coal Co. | 102½ |
| 10 | Lowell Bleachery Co. | 120 |
| 10 | Nash Motors Co. | 109⅝ |
| 5 | National Lead Co. | 145⅝ |
| 10 | Naumkeag Steam Cotton Co. | 176¼ |
| 20 | Punta Alegre Sugar Co. | 50¾ |
| 20 | Standard Oil of Indiana | 57 |
| 20 | Standard Oil of New York | 40¼ |
| 20 | Texas Company | 38⅞ |
| 5 | United Fruit Co. | 195¼ |
| 10 | U.S. Steel Corp. | 97 |
| 15 | West Point Mfg. Co. | 135 |

# Charrette Corporation

"E n Charrette" is an expression used among architectural an design professionals to describe the ordeal of meeting a rush dead line. It's meant to convey an atmosphere where the stakes are high the pace is fast, the time is short, and the slightest error can mea the difference between success and failure. Servicing the needs of this clientele requires a partner that approaches its tasks with the same sense of urgency and precision. This is what the Charrette Corporation has been doing for more than 30 years, and it is why the company continues to grow in the highly competitive world of graphic equipment, supplies, and services.

## Commitment to Inventory, Distribution, and Service

"Our name says it all," says President and CEO John J. Ford III. "We built our business 'En Charrette.' When you have a rush job, we have what you need, and we can get it to you right away." Charrette maintains the largest inventory of design equipment and supplies in the United States, with same-day shipment/next-day delivery as the company standard. The company's product line encompasses nearly 100,000 different items, from modeling and office supplies to state-of-the-art digital imaging and CAD (computer-aided design) printing systems. Taking orders via phone, fax, the Internet, and electronic data interface (EDI), Charrette offers next-day, direct delivery—in most cases, via the company's own trucks. Its 364-page catalog is the industry reference guide for selecting traditional and digital imaging equipment and supplies.

In addition to its extensive commercial products business, Charrette

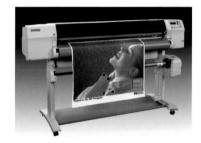

Clockwise from top left: Pictured is an example of digital ink-jet printing, a rapidly growing technology available at Charrette Corporation.

Charrette's management team includes (standing, from left) Richard Johnson, treasurer; John J. Ford III, president and CEO; (seated, from left) Orlando Corsi Jr., chief financial officer; and Nancy Opresnick, vice president, retail division.

Charrette's headquarters is located on Olympia Avenue in Woburn.

outlets also cater to students, fine artists, and general consumers. The company also has a network of reprographic centers offering large-format color output, signage, large color photos, color copying, and blueprinting. As part of its reprographic services, Charrette sets up and manages in-house reprographic centers within large companies, offering the benefits of in-house graphic production without the labor and capital costs.

## Commitment to Support and Partnership

In addition to the industry's best products and services, Charrette's customers enjoy a commitment to outstanding customer support. Long before the term "partnering" entered the business vernacular, Charrette was committed to following industry trends and changes, and helping customers adapt to them. As a result, the company was poised to take advantage of the technology revolution of the 1990s. "While the tools of the design trades have changed," explains Ford, "we're doing the same thing we've always done: providing design professionals with what they need." Armed with this insight,

Charrette is at the leading edge of what's happening in the world of electronic imaging. The company has become a tremendous resource for customers looking for cost-effective, state-of-the-art solutions.

## Commitment to Growth

Charrette aims at nothing less than being the dominant provider of design products and services in the United States through continued development of product lines, enhanced service offerings, enhanced sales and marketing efforts, and geographic acquisition and expansion. In addition to its operations in Boston; Providence; New Haven; New York City; Rochester Buffalo; Philadelphia; Washington D.C.; Detroit; and Chicago, the company has recently acquired operations in San Francisco, Los Angeles, Dayton, Atlanta, and Houston, with an overall aim of doubling in size and becoming a $220 million company by 2002.

As Charrette heads for a role in the national spotlight, the company plans to continue to live up to its name, with a commitment to service, inventory, and partnership with its clients.

ARBER'S TRAVEL SERVICE, INC. HAS ALWAYS BELIEVED that travel is a service business, and for more than 50 years, the company has been providing its corporate and leisure clients with a local, personal touch to ensure a quality travel experience. This philosophy stems from founder and travel industry visionary Bernie Garber,

Dorchester, Massachusetts, native and entrepreneur.

## The Beginning

Garber started in business in 1941 with Garber's Auto Driving School. When he found that many of his driving students sought his advice about vacation destinations in New England, he became a travel agent and, with the assistance of his wife, Bea, opened Garber's Travel Service, Inc. in 1946, using the living room of his Beacon Street apartment in Brookline as his headquarters. The company now maintains its world headquarters at 1047 Commonwealth Avenue in Boston, although a leisure vacation office is still open at the original location.

## Striving for Lifelong Customers

While Garber's Travel Service, Inc. has grown beyond its founder's living room, the company's travel experts still focus on total client satisfaction, and as a result, the company has numerous second- and third-generation clients. "We want to handle the business travel, the annual vacation, the honeymoon and anniversary trips, the retirement experience, and even the children's honeymoon," emphasizes President Lou Garber, who has been involved with his father's business for more than 30 years.

According to *Travel Weekly*, Garber's Travel Service, Inc. has grown to become one of the Top 20 travel management companies in the United States, with more than $257 million in sales and more than 100 locations coast-to-coast in the United States and Canada, as well as in the United Kingdom. While the company's growth is

expected to double in the next three to five years, Lou Garber insists on maintaining the firm's tradition of being a family-owned company and a neighborhood business. Rather than staffing large reservation centers, Garber Travel has peppered New England with local branches and corporate on-site offices that are part of the business and residential communities in which they operate.

## Corporate Travel Services

Garber's Corporate Travel Management Department has earned its distinction by providing its valued clients with the highest level of personalized service, effective strategic planning, strong negotiating power, and leading-edge travel management reporting tools. Clients appreciate Garber Travel's commitment to helping them achieve their corporate goals by providing effective and easy-to-use management information products that help them realize a greater cost efficiency through automation.

GarberMagic 2000 is a Y2K-compliant, Windows-based product that provides the company's corporate clients with access to a comprehensive travel management reporting and query system, allowing travel managers and controllers the ability to analyze their travel patterns effectively. It also enables them to access up-to-date, specific information necessary in the development and implementation of a stringent travel policy.

Garber also offers its corporate clients an after-hours Emergency Travel Service, which operates 24 hours a day, seven days a week, from the Schrafft Center in Charlestown, as well as a Meetings & Incentive Management Group.

## Into the Future— A Tradition of Service in a Changing World

As the millennium approaches, Garber Travel is able to offer its leisure and corporate clients access to the future and the ability to request on-line vacation, air, car, hotel, and cruise reservations via its Web site—http://www.garber.com. The company's Magic Carpet Vacations division creates exciting, affordable vacation packages for singles, couples, and families.

Garber Travel believes that its most important assets are the people inside its more than 100 offices. It is with great pride that Garber boasts of its more than 400 employees, of whom 180 have been with the company for more than five years, 100 have been with the company for more than 10 years, and 18 have been part of the Garber team for more than 20 years.

Garber is the largest travel company in New England. Although it may not be the largest agency in the world, when it comes to the quality of its service and the knowledge and expertise of its travel professionals, Garber's Travel Service, Inc. is "Number One."

PICTURED HERE IS THE GARBER'S TRAVEL SERVICE, INC. STAFF AT THE FIRM'S DOWNTOWN BOSTON OFFICE AT ONE INTERNATIONAL PLACE.

ALLAN E. DINES

**T**HE STORY OF WBZ-TV AND RADIO IS THE STORY OF BROADcasting—a story of community, diversity, innovation, and quality. From the early days of radio, when WBZ was the first station to warn listeners of an impending hurricane, to the first television broadcasts 50 years ago that brought images from around the country and the world right into New England living rooms,

WBZ-TV 4 and NewsRadio 1030 have successfully combined an extraordinary mix of innovation and tradition that generations of New Englanders have grown to trust.

### Television Firsts

**W**BZ-TV is now on the air!" proclaimed news anchor Arch MacDonald on June 9th, 1948. Since laying the cornerstone for its broadcast center on Soldiers Field Road, the legacy of WBZ 4 has been rooted in a number of remarkable firsts. In its first year of operation alone, WBZ brought New England its first Major League Baseball game, World Championship boxing match, college football game, Republican and Democratic National Conventions, and the Presidential Inauguration of Harry S. Truman. The experienced News 4 New England team, many of whom have been with the station for decades and hail from New England, bring continuity, perspective, and a regional familiarity that is unparalleled in New England.

### News Is a Public Service

**W**BZ has always found its strength and success in the fabric of New England. In

1948, the station launched the country's first public service campaign on television. WBZ's "For Kid's Sake," launched in 1978, also broke new ground as the country's first nationally syndicated campaign. The station has continued to initiate campaigns on a wide variety of community concerns from AIDS to supporting the arts, motivating New Englanders to take action. The long-running "Stop the Violence" campaign, which puts the breadth of the station's resources behind an effort to increase awareness of violence issues in the home, in schools, and on the streets, has set a new standard for public service. In 1981, anchor Jack Williams teamed up with the Massachusetts Adoption Resource Exchange to create "Wednesday's Child," a weekly series that helps to place hard to adopt children in good homes. The "Wednesday's Child" program has found homes for over 400 local children. WBZ's leadership in public service has inspired stations all over the country to emulate its award-winning nationally syndicated campaigns as models of community excellence.

### A New England Tradition

**A**s it continues to bring milestone events to New England including the closing of the historic Boston Garden and the first ever broadcast of the Boston Symphony Orchestra's Youth Concerts; as it ushers in advances such as digital television, the Internet, and Web TV, WBZ is destined to remain a vital information source for all of New England. While new technology in the next millennium promises to change television as we know it, New England viewers can rely on the WBZ tradition of community, diversity, innovation, and quality for decades to come.

CLOCKWISE FROM TOP: NEWS 4 NEW ENGLAND'S LEAD ANCHOR TEAM INCLUDES (FROM LEFT) LIZ WALKER, BOB LOBEL, ED CARROLL, JOE SHORTSLEEVE, AND JOYCE KULHAWIK.

SUZANNE BATES (LEFT) AND SCOTT WAHLE COHOST WBZ 4'S PREMIER MORNING PROGRAM, "NEWS 4 THIS MORNING," WEEKDAYS FROM 5 TO 8 A.M.

THE NEWS 4 NEW ENGLAND TEAM AT WBZ 4 INCLUDES (FROM LEFT) JOHN HENNING, JOYCE KULHAWIK, BOB LOBEL, VIRGINIA CHA, JACK WILLIAMS, LIZ WALKER, JOE SHORTSLEEVE, ED CARROLL, JOE BERGANTINO, AND PAULA LYONS.

◀ ED MALITSKY

I N AN EVER CHANGING POLITICAL AND ECONOMIC CLIMATE, WBZ NewsRadio 1030 remains as relevant today as when radio broadcasts first began. Whether at home, at the office, in the car, or on foot, listeners can tune into what has become a New England institution to get the latest news, sports, weather, and traffic information. Although the radio industry has been fraught with constantly

changing formats, WBZ remains consistent and familiar. The station's core team—Gil Santos and Gary LaPierre, who have been together for more than 25 years—are joined by veteran journalists Deb Lawler, Gary McQuaide, Anthony Silva, and Diane Stern. Well-known talk show host David Brudnoy has become a nighttime staple for thousands of New Englanders. Like its sister television station WBZ-TV 4, WBZ NewsRadio 1030 has become vital to the fabric of the region and continues to make significant contributions to the community it serves.

## New England's First Radio Station

When the station signed on, on September 19, 1921, from the Eastern States Exposition in Springfield, Massachusetts, it became New England's first radio station. Originally owned by Westinghouse Broadcasting Company, the station's early broadcasts originated from the Westinghouse plant in East Springfield. Programming included a variety of live music—mostly classical and opera—along with farm and agricultural reports, baseball scores, and talks by local politicians. Westinghouse remained the owner of WBZ until it purchased CBS Inc. in 1997 and adopted the new corporate moniker—the CBS Corporation.

WBZ opened a Boston studio in the Hotel Brunswick in 1924, and three years later moved to the Statler Hotel. In 1948, the station, along with the new WBZ-TV station, relocated to its new broadcast center on Soldiers Field Road, where it remains today.

## Setting Precedents

Throughout its history, WBZ Radio has been a precedent-setting news outlet. The station aired the first radio broadcast of the Boston Marathon in April 1931, and in 1933, was the first Boston station to have a staff meteorologist. When a hurricane hit the area in 1938, WBZ was the first station to warn listeners of the impending storm, helping to save countless lives. WBZ was also the first station to air school cancellations in 1926, and has been the flagship broadcaster for the legendary Boston Bruins NHL hockey team since 1994.

Concern for the community and active participation have been ongoing commitments for the station and its personnel. WBZ received both a commendation from the U.S. Coast Guard and a letter of thanks from the White House in 1976 when traffic reporter Joe Green, while flying in the WBZ traffic helicopter, rescued a young man from the Merrimack River after his kayak capsized.

Like Green, the station itself has been there for the community in times of need. In 1955, WBZ began the 700 Fund, a fund-raising campaign held in conjunction with the Salvation Army's Christmas appeal. In 1980, WBZ Radio began the Children's Hospital Fund drive, which has become an annual event. Three years later, the drive was expanded to a telethon broadcast on both WBZ Radio and WBZ-TV 4. Together, the stations have raised

more than $11 million for the hospital since beginning the broadcasts in 1983.

Within the industry and New England, WBZ has been recognized for its broadcast achievements and community service. Recent awards include the 1995 and 1998 National Association of Broadcasters' Marconi Award for Excellence in Broadcasting, Major Market Station of the Year, and the Edward R. Murrow Award for Excellence in Electronic Journalism in 1995 and 1996.

Since 1992, WBZ has offered an all-news format for daily programming, and in 1998, the station expanded to include weekends. With a history of strength in this format, WBZ NewsRadio 1030 continues its 75-plus-year tradition of award-winning programming.

LYNN MCCANN

CLOCKWISE FROM TOP LEFT: WBZ NEWSRADIO'S NUMBER-ONE-RATED MORNING NEWS IS ANCHORED BY (FROM LEFT) GIL SANTOS, DEB LAWLER, AND GARY LAPIERRE.

NEW ENGLAND'S MOST POPULAR TALK RADIO PERSONALITIES (FROM LEFT), BOB RALEIGH AND DAVID BRUDNOY, BROADCAST THEIR PROGRAMS WEEKNIGHTS ON WBZ NEWSRADIO.

PICTURED HERE IN FRONT OF THE STATE HOUSE, WBZ NEWSRADIO'S MOBILE STUDIO CAN BE SEEN ALL OVER NEW ENGLAND COVERING THE NEWS OF THE REGION.

ERIC ROTH

O N THE SURFACE, THE CITIES OF BOSTON AND MIAMI DON'T HAV
much in common, starting with fall foliage versus palm trees. Y
in 1993, Sunbeam Television Corporation's owner and presiden
Edmund Ansin, took the winning formula of the company
WSVN television station in Miami and applied it to Boston
WHDH-TV Channel 7. The result has been a successful turr

around of the once-struggling local station.

The privately owned Sunbeam Television purchased Boston's WHDH-TV (then known as WNEV-TV, an affiliate of CBS) from the New England TV Corporation in April 1993. The station was the last locally owned television network affiliate in Boston at the time and the city's second television station, debuting on June 21, 1948, as WNAC-TV, two weeks after WBZ-TV 4.

### Finding a Niche in Boston

When it was purchased by Sunbeam, Channel 7's news operation ranked third in both viewership and overall sales revenue. Ansin knew that the station needed to be repositioned, and that its target audience had to be redefined in order to pick up younger viewers. Guided by a corporate philosophy that the television business should focus on contemporary values and interests, Sunbeam then set about tailoring the formula of Miami's WSVN for the Boston market. Along with a change in presentation, fundamental alterations in content and pacing were implemented, as well as extensive upgrading of equipment, including satellite trucks, microwave vans, and studio editing facilities.

Under the new call letters WHDH, the nightly 7 News debute as content-based and fast-paced broadcasts aimed at creating a unique, local image. Newscasts were filled with on-site reports, and local reporters were sent to cover national news stories. The newscasts also featured contemporary, new graphics, while the anchor delivered the news in a bustling newsroom setting abuzz with report ers scurrying in the background.

In another bold move, WHDH decided in January 1994 to pre-empt the *CBS Morning News* with four hours of local news programming in the 5 to 9 a.m. time slot. That established the station as the

LEFT: IN 1993, SUNBEAM TELEVISION CORPORATION'S OWNER AND PRESIDENT, EDMUND ANSIN, TOOK THE WINNING FORMULA OF THE COMPANY'S WSVN TELEVISION STATION IN MIAMI AND APPLIED IT TO BOSTON'S WHDH-TV CHANNEL 7.

RIGHT: THE AWARD-WINNING ON-AIR JOURNALISTS AT 7 NEWS INCLUDE (FROM LEFT) CHIEF METEOROLOGIST HARVEY LEONARD, ANCHOR RANDY PRICE, ANCHOR KIM CARRIGAN, AND SPORTS DIRECTOR GENE LAVANCHY.

LUCY COBOS PHOTOGRAPHY

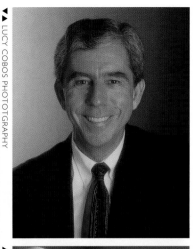

LUCY COBOS PHOTOTGRAPHY

CLOCKWISE FROM TOP LEFT: THE 7 WEATHER TEAM INCLUDES (FROM LEFT)METEOROLOGISTS TODD GROSS AND MISH MICHAELS, AND CHIEF METEOROLOGIST HARVEY LEONARD.

MICHAEL CARSON SERVES AS GENERAL MANAGER OF WHDH-TV.

THE 7 NEWS INVESTIGATORS FEATURES REPORTER HANK PHILLIPPI-RYAN'S INVESTIGATIONS OF CONSUMER ISSUES. IN 1989, PHILLIPPI-RYAN WAS NAMED PRINCIPAL REPORTER FOR THE STATION'S AWARD-WINNING INVESTIGATIVE UNIT.

THE 7 NEWS HEALTHCAST IS HOSTED BY LESTER STRONG, A 15-YEAR VETERAN AT THE STATION WHO WON THE PRESTIGIOUS WILLIAM A. HINTON AWARD BY THE MASSACHUSETTS DEPARTMENT OF PUBLIC HEALTH IN 1994 (LEFT).

VETERAN ANALYST ANDY HILLER HEADS THE 7 NEWS POLITICAL TEAM (RIGHT).

ly one in the Boston market th its own full morning news-st. Later that year, WHDH came an NBC affiliate. The ove enabled the station to lever-e the programming advantages being affiliated with the num-r one prime-time network, with ows such as *Today, NBC Nightly ws*, and *The Tonight Show* star-g Andover native Jay Leno, ng with NBC's strong sports verage.

As a result, WHDH has become auded pacesetter in local news verage, and is commonly referred as 7 News. It was named the st TV News Station in *Boston agazine*'s 1998 Best of Boston ards.

**xperienced Anchors, ommunity-First Coverage**

he award-winning on-air journalists at 7 News are aded by the weekday prime-time m of Randy Price, a longtime oston anchor, and Kim Carrigan, no joined Channel 7 in 1994. ston Magazine named Carrigan st TV News Anchor in its 1998 st of Boston issue. Sportscaster ene Lavanchy joined the station 1993, while Chief Meteorologist arvey Leonard—who, like vanchy and Carrigan, was the

recipient of awards from *Boston Magazine*—has been with Channel 7 since 1977.

Sunbeam has made the interest of the Boston community its top priority since its 1993 acquisition of the station. Through survey groups with viewers, 7 News has identified its viewers' three areas of news interest—personal health issues, family and children concerns, and consumer watchdog information. In response, certain features were added to the nightly 7 News broadcasts, such as the 7 Healthcast segment, hosted by Lester Strong, a 15-year veteran at the station who won the Massachusetts Department of Public

Health's prestigious William A. Hinton Award in 1994. Another segment, The 7 News Investigators, features reporter Hank Phillippi-Ryan's investigations of consumer issues. Phillippi-Ryan joined the news team in 1983 as a general-assignment reporter, and in 1989 was named principal reporter for the station's award-winning investigative unit. Veteran analyst Andy Hiller heads the news' political team.

A recent complement to 7 News programming is the *Weather Almanac*, a publication created by the 7 Weather Team in conjunction with the National Weather Service, several local organizations, and top scientists. Information from the almanac is also available on the station's Web site (www.whdh.com), which features breaking news, sports, and weather from the news team.

With a bold presence in the Boston area, 7 News is certain to continue its leadership role among local broadcasters, delivering news and information to future generations well into the new millennium.

# The Stubbins Associates

**C**ELEBRATING ITS 50TH ANNIVERSARY IN 1999, THE STUBBIN Associates (TSA) is a world-renowned planning and design fir based in Cambridge, Massachusetts. One of the few organization to have won the coveted Architectural Firm Award from th American Institute of Architects, TSA has become known f such notable work as Citicorp Center in Manhattan, th

Landmark Tower in Yokohama (the tallest building in Japan), and Boston's Federal Reserve Bank, and in the process has won more than 150 design awards for planning, architecture, and interior design.

TSA is distinguished not only by the quality of its work, but by the breadth of its portfolio and client base. The firm has produced successful projects that have included high-rise office towers, mixed-use commercial developments, college and university projects, high-tech biomedical research laboratories, medical centers, hotels and resorts, and even award-winning jails. For the U.S. government, TSA has designed the U.S. Embassy in Singapore, the Federal Medical Center at Fort Devens, and the Ronald Reagan Presidential Library in Simi Valley. Clients have included Citicorp, Mitsubishi, Harvard University, Massachusetts General Hospital, Lotus Development Corporation, and Bristol-Myers Squibb.

ONE OF THE FEW ORGANIZATIONS TO HAVE WON THE COVETED ARCHITECTURAL FIRM AWARD FROM THE AMERICAN INSTITUTE OF ARCHITECTS, THE STUBBINS ASSOCIATES (TSA) IS KNOWN FOR SUCH NOTABLE WORK AS THE LANDMARK TOWER (TOP) IN YOKOHAMA (THE TALLEST BUILDING IN JAPAN) AND CITICORP CENTER (BOTTOM) IN MANHATTAN.

Bosto

Around Boston, TSA is well known for such projects as the Countway Library at the Harvard Medical School, the innovative Pusey Library in Harvard Yard, headquarters for Lotus Development Corporation, the Charles Street Jail, the Federal Reserve Bank, the new Seaport Hotel and Conference Center, the Marriott Hotel at Copley Place, the Omnimax Theater at the Museum of Science, and the BioSquare II research laboratory at the Boston Medical Center. TSA has also completed multiple projects at the Cushing Academy, Massachusetts Institute of Technology, and Boston University's Charles River campus.

Led by eight principals, each with special expertise, TSA continually strives to break new ground. Current projects include a major repositioning of the former Sands Hotel & Casino property in Las Vegas as the Venetian. When complete, it will be the world's largest resort hotel and casino, comprising 6,000 hotel suites. TSA was the architect of record for the redesign of Massachusetts General Hospital to support its new mission of patient-focused care. TSA is also the executive architect for the International Medical Center in Beirut, and is the design architect for a major new museum in Indianapolis for the Indiana Historical Society. Current or recent work in the academic sector includes projects at Harvard University, University of Delaware, North Carolina State University, Northern Michigan University, University of Minnesota, Bryant College, Fairfield University, Carleton College, University of Chicago, and Vanderbilt University.

TSA's comprehensive professional services embrace planning, architecture and urban design, interiors, landscape design, and signage and graphics. The firm is both design and technology driven— all professional staff are computer literate, and construction documents are 100 percent CAD-produced. TSA also maintains a full-service model shop that works in a variety of media.

The Stubbins Associates has a proud past and an even more interesting future. As one of the country's most innovative and honored architectural firms, TSA is poised to be even more successful in the next 50 years.

▶ KEVIN BURKE

▶ WARREN JAGGER

TSA IS DISTINGUISHED NOT ONLY BY THE QUALITY OF ITS WORK, BUT BY THE BREADTH OF ITS PORTFOLIO AND CLIENT BASE. THE FIRM HAS PRODUCED SUCCESSFUL PROJECTS THAT HAVE INCLUDED HIGH-RISE OFFICE TOWERS, MIXED-USE COMMERCIAL DEVELOPMENTS, COLLEGE AND UNIVERSITY PROJECTS, HIGH-TECH BIOMEDICAL RESEARCH LABORATORIES, MEDICAL CENTERS, HOTELS AND RESORTS, AND EVEN AWARD-WINNING JAILS.

EVERAGING ITS EXPERTISE IN RADIO FREQUENCY (RF) AN[D] microwave technology, M/A-COM, a division of AM[P] Incorporated, spent the early 1990s transforming itself from [a] defense-related company into a commercial business poise[d] to become a key player in the emerging wireless marke[t.] M/A-COM today is the world's largest noncaptive suppli[er]

of RF/microwave components and subsystems.

Headquartered in Lowell, M/A-COM's products—which include a variety of semiconductors, active and control components, and multifunction assemblies, among a host of other items—are used around the globe by Fortune 500 customers in the wireless, telecommunications, automotive, aerospace, and defense markets.

M/A-COM has 1.5 million square feet of operations space around the world, with more than 20 manufacturing locations worldwide, including Lowell, Waltham, Watertown, Amesbury, and Burlington in Massachusetts. In addition, the company has sales offices in 33 countries. M/A-COM employs nearly 4,000 people, including more than 300 degreed engineers. In 1998, the *Boston Business Journal* ranked M/A-COM

as the eighth-largest corporate em[-]ployer in Middlesex County base[d] on total number of employees.

### One-Stop Shop

M/A-COM was founded in Boston in 1950 as Microwav[e] Associates by four former enginee[rs] from Sylvania. From the beginning, the company's strategy was to grow by acquisition, buying up many of the small companies

M/A-COM, A DIVISION OF AMP INCORPORATED, IS HEADQUARTERED IN LOWELL. ITS PRODUCTS ARE USED BY FORTUNE 500 CUSTOMERS IN THE WIRELESS, TELECOMMUNICATIONS, AUTOMOTIVE, AEROSPACE, AND DEFENSE MARKETS.

that populated the microwave industry at the time. The goal was to create a one-stop shop in the RF/microwave community. In 1957, the company moved out of the city, building a 50,000-square-foot facility in Burlington. That year, the company also made its first public offering.

After launching Microwave Associates Ltd. in England in the early 1960s and making a series of acquisitions during the 1970s, the company changed its name to M/A-COM in 1978 to reflect the expansion from microwave to communications systems. In the early 1970s, the company's shares began trading on the New York Stock Exchange.

In 1984, M/A-COM unveiled a state-of-the-art gallium arsenide semiconductor fabrication plant in Lowell. A pioneer in this silicon alternative, M/A-COM was one of the first companies to invest heavily in volume gallium arsenide. Through more acquisitions in the 1980s, M/A-COM filled out the breadth and depth of its product lines by entering the expanding RF interconnection market, as well as expanding its customer base in the space and intelligence applications areas. Through the vertical integration of its acquired product line, M/A-COM offered added value to its customers.

As the 1980s came to an end, so did the cold war, thus launching an era in which M/A-COM and other companies in the defense industry would be forced to diversify their product offerings. Thus began M/A-COM's transformation, reengineering, and reorganization to address the commercial market. As wireless technology came into the mainstream, M/A-COM's revenues from the private sector increased. Today, about 70 percent of M/A-COM's sales are from commercial markets.

In June 1995, M/A-COM was acquired by AMP Inc., a Harrisburg, Pennsylvania-based manufacturer of electrical/electronic interconnection products, with annual sales around $6 billion. "AMP wanted to grow into the next century as a total interconnection solutions

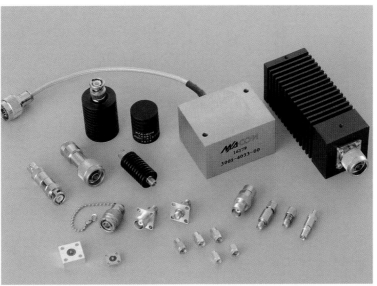

company," says Phillipe Lemaitre, AMP corporate vice president and head of the Advanced Technologies Group, which includes M/A-COM. "Wireless is an interconnection technology. M/A-COM was poised to give AMP a quick jump into the market."

M/A-COM now forms the cornerstone of the Global Wireless Products Group within AMP. The division's products support applications that include cellular telephones and networks, telemetry, and other mobile data applications; wireless local-loop, broadband community antenna television (CATV); wireless local-area networks; satellite communications; vehicle sensors; navigation; and radar.

## Leading the Way into the Future

As M/A-COM enters the next millennium, the division will continue to operate based on three key business principles: investing in emerging technologies; enhancing high-volume manufacturing processes; and recruiting, developing, and retaining people.

As an example of its commitment to manufacturing, M/A-COM in May 1998 opened a 60,000-square-foot electronic manufacturing plant in Cork, Ireland. The facility designs and manufactures products for cellular phones, cable television delivery systems, direct broadcast satellite applications, and the industrial and automotive sensor market.

The automotive market is also a good example of how M/A-COM will leverage its knowledge in new and far-reaching wireless applications. Today, M/A-COM is supplying radar devices to Mercedes and other high-end automakers. "We took an idea used in military jets and applied it to the family sedan," says Lemaitre.

## Global Reach, Local Roots

Although the company has clients and facilities around the world, it is still an active member of the Merrimack Valley business community. In July 1991, M/A-COM established M/A-COM Food Share, Inc., a nonprofit subsidiary that continues to develop programs to meet the food assistance needs of families in the Merrimack Valley and southern New Hampshire areas. Food Share both gathers and grows food. For example, to reach out to Merrimack Valley's Cambodian population, Food Share grows food native to that country. In addition to contributing financially, M/A-COM employees donate their services to the program. The company also contributes to the United Way Fund, various community and educational institutions, and other charitable organizations.

With a huge investment in research and development, a global reach, and a concern for the communities in which it is located, M/A-COM continues to be on the frontier of new wireless applications and products.

M/A-COM's products include RF semiconductors and a wide variety of wireless components and assemblies.

A MERICA'S INFORMATION TECHNOLOGY (IT) MARKET IS THE world's largest, accounting for 45 percent of the world's total IT spending. Serving the needs of this demanding market is a daunting task, and not for those who accept limitations or harbor reservations. What's needed is a company that believes that everything is possible and that has the people, resources,

and track record to back the claim.

Enter Bull Americas, a division of Paris-based Bull Worldwide Information Systems. Located in the Boston suburb of Billerica, the Bull Americas headquarters is the nerve center from which the company serves the IT needs of the Western Hemisphere. Bull provides solutions that cover the entire IT spectrum, including PCs, mainframes, software solutions, legacy enterprise servers, open client/server networks, enterprise management and security, smart cards, and systems integration services. In the public sector, Bull's IT solutions are an integral part of the operations of 41 state governments, 150 public agencies, 60 municipalities, and numerous educational institutions. In the commercial sector, Bull solutions play a prominent role in the health care, financial services, and telecommunications industries.

Bull's strength goes beyond the size of its markets and its cutting-edge technologies. To understand the company's growth, it is necessary to understand the company's philosophy of the creation and development of information systems.

## Tailoring the Solution to the Enterprise

K ey to Bull's success is the realization that customers are not interested in technology for technology's sake. They are looking to better understand and serve their end customer, they are looking to improve their internal processes, and they are looking for better ways to control the flow of information and convert it into measurable business results. Bull believes that information systems have a twofold purpose: as an investment

in business performance and an investment in progress.

Since every business is unique and has a unique set of priorities, Bull views the development of a customer's information system as an evolutionary process. The first step of this process involves listening to and understanding the customer's present and future requirements. The second step is to propose a solution, and the final step is to take responsibility for the implementation of the system. When Bull designs and implements a system, technology is put in the service of the user rather than the other way around.

## Solutions for the Public Sector

S tate and local governments represent Bull's largest single market segment. In an era when budgetary restraint is the watchword, the public sector faces the dilemma of growing responsibilities and shrinking budgets. Bull is meeting the challenge with innovative solutions that enhance both productivity and service.

The State of Michigan was one of the first to move its citizens out of traditional Medicaid and into managed care. The transition—which affected 1.2 million Michigan citizens—was in the hands of the state's Medical Services Administration (MSA). The organization's reliable but aging mainframe computers produced static, dated reports, requiring anywhere from one week to three months to generate them. In the words of one official, "It was costing us more to extract data than the data was worth."

What was needed was a system with real-time reporting capability, one that supplied up-to-the-minute comprehensive information on every aspect of MSA's operations. According to one MSA director,

GEORGE MCNEIL, PRESIDENT AND CEO OF BULL AMERICAS, BELIEVES BULL IS WELL POSITIONED FOR STRONG GROWTH IN THE UNITED STATES AND THROUGHOUT THE WESTERN HEMISPHERE.

COMPANIES LIKE INTERMEDIA COMMUNICATIONS INC. OF TAMPA—ONE OF THE COUNTRY'S FASTEST-GROWING TELECOMMUNICATIONS CARRIERS—HAVE CHOSEN OPENMASTER, BULL'S ENTERPRISE MANAGEMENT AND SECURITY SYSTEM, TO MANAGE THEIR NETWORKS.

We had very rigid requirements which other potential bidders didn't want to commit themselves. Bull was the only bidder that believed it could develop a system that met our specifications."

Today, the reports that once took weeks to create now can be generated in 10 minutes to an hour, and the State of Michigan has realized reductions of up to 25 percent in administrative and Medicaid recovery costs. The flexibility of the system also allows MSA to deal with the broader issue of health care service analysis. For instance, quarterly managed care report cards are generated for the 4,000 primary care physicians under MSA's jurisdiction, allowing MSA to evaluate physician performance.

The success of Bull's solution for MSA caught the attention of other Michigan state agencies, and this, in turn, has led to a five-year contract with the state to create an on-line decision support system.

## Solutions for the Private Sector

Private sector health care providers have also had to keep up with the migration to managed care. Health Alliance Plan (HAP) is one of the largest health maintenance organizations (HMOs) in the country, serving 530,000 members in 3,500 employer groups across Michigan and Ohio. Paradoxically, the organization's strong reputation and resulting growth became a concern, as existing computer resources strained to keep up with the growing subscriber base. Today, a Bull dual DPS9000 mainframe handles all mission-critical applica-

tions, including billing, claims, underwriting, care management, and membership. Dennis Sirosky, chief information officer for HAP, notes that HAP couldn't operate without its Bull mainframe. He also adds, "Bull's level of support has always exceeded our expectations. They go out of their way to assist us."

In the information age, what really counts is getting the right information—that is, the information needed to make the right business decisions. This is what Bull does for all of its clients. Everything is possible, and Bull solutions enhance the possibilities.

BULL'S SOLUTIONS FOR THE PUBLIC SECTOR (STATE AND LOCAL GOVERNMENT) CAN BE FOUND IN 41 STATES AND 150 AGENCIES. BULL FOCUSES ITS INFORMATION TECHNOLOGY SOLUTIONS IN FOUR KEY AREAS: HEALTH AND HUMAN SERVICES; EDUCATION; TAX AND TREASURY; AND CRIMINAL JUSTICE/PUBLIC SAFETY. BULL'S OTHER KEY VERTICAL MARKETS ARE TELECOMMUNICATIONS AND FINANCIAL SERVICES.

IN THE FRENETICALLY PACED HIGH-TECHNOLOGY MARKET, HIRING—and keeping—the best and brightest talent is crucial for staying o the cutting edge and maintaining a competitive advantage. With mo than 6,000 employees worldwide, annual sales surpassing $1 billio and leadership in each of the markets it serves, Teradyne Inc. h clearly found a recipe for success. The company, which designs an produces test systems used in manufacturing virtually all of today's electronics, offers its employees an entrepreneurial environment, a nonhierarchical management structure based on learning by doing, a commitment to quality, and facilities in cities that are great places to work and live, including the company's Boston headquarters.

"Boston is an environment where Teradyne—and our employees—has been able to grow," says George Chamillard, president and CEO. "In the technology industry, you need professional growth and growth as an individual. You can't find a better place to keep expanding your technical skills than Boston, and it's probably one of the top 10 cities in the world in terms of music, drama, sports, and education. People stay here because they can grow."

That's also one reason they stay at Teradyne, where employees can find autonomy, diversity, and entrepreneurial opportunity. "If you're an engineer who's just out of school, do you want to spend time working in Europe or the Far East? Do you want to be in engineering, technical management, or sales?" Chamillard asks. "Teradyne has all of those jobs."

### A Progressive Management Approach

Unlike many large companies, Teradyne has resisted the pitfalls of bureaucracy by fostering a flexible work environment marked by open offices and few titles. This approach has helped eliminate traditional barriers between management and staff, effectively keeping the "knowledge power" close to the customer. Says David Leip, a design engineer in the Industrial Consumer Division in Boston, "My engineering manager is always available to provide guidance, but the individual engineer is in charge of making sure the project is com- pleted. There's no politics. We all work together."

The company's progressive management approach has paid off for its customers, employees, and stockholders, as sales have doubled in the past five years alon "We believe you build a business by getting into the mud with the customer and understanding the problems they have at a detailed level," says Chamillard. "And whil you're down in the mud, you hop you find a kernel of gold."

Teradyne's first kernel of gold, the creation of automatic test equipment (ATE), actually launchec an entire industry. ATE was the forward-looking vision of founder Alex d'Arbeloff and Nick DeWolf, who were Massachusetts Institute of Technology (MIT) classmates in the late 1940s. The men founde Teradyne in 1960, and set up shop in rented space above Joe and Nemo hot-dog stand in downtown Bostor In 1961, they sold their first prod- uct, a diode tester, to Raytheon Company. Teradyne has since focused on expanding its semicon-

ctor test business, while extend-
g its reach into new markets. The
mpany became publicly held in
70, and its stock has been listed
the New York Stock Exchange
ce 1979.

Today, Teradyne is a diversified
ganization and the world's largest
pplier of ATE for the electronics
d telecommunications industries.
products are used to test semi-
nductors, circuit assemblies, tele-
one lines, networks, computerized
ecommunications systems, and
ftware. Teradyne also produces
ck-plane assemblies and high-
nsity connectors used in high-
rformance electronic systems.

the third-largest manufacturing
ployer in Boston, the company
s additional manufacturing facili-
s in Agoura Hills, San Jose, and
alnut Creek, California; Deerfield,
inois; Nashua, New Hampshire;
ublin, Ireland; and Kumamoto,
pan.

## History of Growth

eradyne's growth over the
years has been fueled by both
quisitions and internal develop-
ent. By establishing a series of
art-up companies, Teradyne has
en able to enter new markets and
fer entrepreneurial opportunities
employees. In 1996, through a
nt venture with MIT Corporation
e governing body of Massachu-
tts Institute of Technology), the
mpany formed Kinetrix, marking
e most recent success story in
eradyne's ongoing affiliation with
IT. Located in Bedford, New
ampshire, the subsidiary builds
echanical manufacturing equip-

ment for the semiconductor test
industry, a new arena for Teradyne.

Complementing his current
duties as Teradyne's chairman,
d'Arbeloff assumed the same post
at MIT Corporation in 1997. He
was also the driving force behind
Teradyne's total quality management (TQM) initiative in 1990,
which focused on customer satisfac-

tion and continuous improvement.
The company credits TQM as a
major factor in its recent accom-
plishments in new product development, operations efficiency, and
sales and earnings growth.

In recognition of its achievements, Teradyne has received numerous honors, including the *Boston
Globe*'s 1996 Company of the Year
award. And in July 1998, for the
10th consecutive year, Teradyne
was named one of the 10 best
manufacturers for test and material
handling equipment by VLSI
Research.

Looking to the future, Teradyne
expects to mine more kernels of
gold in new market areas, such as
computer telephony, networking,
and software testing. The company
has also made recent investments
in emerging technologies. "We
bought five companies in different
segments of software testing," says
Chamillard. "We're using that as a
lens to get close to our customers,
to see if we can do something that
will be great. I think we will."

"BOSTON IS AN ENVIRONMENT WHERE
TERADYNE—AND OUR EMPLOYEES—
HAS BEEN ABLE TO GROW," SAYS
GEORGE CHAMILLARD, PRESIDENT
AND CEO. "YOU CAN'T FIND A BETTER
PLACE TO KEEP EXPANDING YOUR TECH-
NICAL SKILLS THAN BOSTON."

# Papa Gino's Holdings Corporation, Inc.

I N 1961, THE VALERIO FAMILY OPENED ITS FIRST RESTAURAN (Piece O' Pizza) in East Boston, knowing that the food and servic they offered would be the very best. Their dedication to servic together with a selection of traditional recipes, both originating i Italy, soon proved to be the ideal combination that delighted the customers in America. Continuing to perfect their business system

CLOCKWISE FROM TOP:
PAPA GINO'S HOLDINGS CORPORATION, INC. INTRODUCED D'ANGELO/PAPA GINO'S PIZZA EXPRESS AS A DUAL CONCEPT UNIT.

THE D'ANGELO STEAK & CHEESE SUB IS A NUMBER ONE SELLER.

PICTURED HERE IS A TRADITIONAL PAPA GINO'S FREESTANDING UNIT.

they increasingly attracted customers to their restaurant by providing a family atmosphere and authentic Italian dishes. In 1968, they changed the name to Papa Gino's and began expanding throughout the Boston area. To this day, the company continues to be privately owned and operated with executive offices located in Dedham.

### Growing to a Leadership Position in New England

Papa Gino's adheres to the basic principles of quality and service. The company values clean restaurants and employs people committed to pleasing their customers. These founding principles have enabled Papa Gino's to expand to 175 neighborhood restaurants and to assume its now dominant position among Italian-theme quick service restaurants in New England.

While dominance is largely a function of the number of successful operating restaurants, leadership is a more difficult quality to measure. Leadership must be designated and earned through consistent practice of the highest standards of excellence and principle. Papa Gino's has demonstrated its leadership quality through its countless superior interactions with customers, employees, suppliers, landlords, lenders, neighborhoods, and community members.

### Compatible Combination with D'Angelo Sandwich Shops

As a leader in its industry, Papa Gino's Holdings Corporation, Inc. has had many opportunities to form partnerships and business collaborations. When D'Angelo Sandwich Shops became an acquisition possibility, Papa Gino's quickly decided to align itself with the premier regional sub sandwich chain renowned for a long-standing commitment to quality, service, and value in one of the fastest-growing segments of the restaurant industry. Brian McLaughlin had started his company in the Boston area in 1967 as Ma Riva's. Later he was joined by his brother Chip and Jay Howland, and they changed the name to Angelo and then added the letter D—for "delicious." Since that time, D'Angelo Sandwich Shops has grown to more than

200 sandwich shops by following the same basic principles as Papa Gino's.

### Serving 50 Million Guests per Year

The addition of the innovative team of executives and franchisees from D'Angelo (the team that pioneered fresh salads and Syrian pockets in the quick service lunch business) has created a combination that provides unparallele quality choices in the quick service restaurant industry. Papa Gino's has entered a stage where the searc for exciting new product offerings to stay ahead of the changes in customer taste preferences, is continuing at a rapid pace. Primo Pizza, a premium value gourmet meal, value meals, and sandwich wraps all show promise for building customer delight and same-store sales.

Today, in addition to their traditional restaurants, Papa Gino's and D'Angelo have moved closer than ever before to their customer by providing outlets in the region' professional sports stadiums, school hospitals, convention centers, or wherever people in need of a great meal in a family atmosphere gathe Altogether, the company now serves more than 50 million guests per year.

### A Team Dedicated to Service

Customer loyalty closely parallels the firm's employee loyalty. "Our guests tell us in taste tes after taste test that our products and services are the best. That's why so many guests become like family, returning again and again. In addition, our employees becom part of our family, and frequently brother-and-sister, mother-and-son or husband-and-wife combination assist us through the years in the

ntinual building of the business," ates Chief Executive Officer Tom alligan. The company culture, hich is characterized by high values, a strong work ethic, and the ir treatment of people, includes arge number of employees who ve literally spent their entire working lives in these restaurants, keeping the passion for excellence alive.

A simple and lean corporate anagement structure, with a priary focus on guests, spearheads e nearly 7,000 employees toward e company's mission to be the ading multiconcept restaurant ain in New England. "Because e are mindful that this loyal corps our greatest asset, we make every fort to nurture and enhance their lents through our extensive training and development programs, hich constantly refine their skills. hrough mutual respect and recogion, the very special relationship tween our company, our family embers, and our guests floures," Galligan adds.

## Tradition of Community volvement

As a company that recognizes and thrives on its family orieitation, Papa Gino's is devoted being a good neighbor and comssionate citizen. "We have the od fortune to be successful and e able to share that success within e communities where we live and ork," says Galligan. "We proudly onsor Fire Safety Month each ctober with local firehouses; onsor many town athletic teams; ntribute significantly to Easter als; support community fundisers; and have raised more than million for the Genesis Fund. 'e also have been honored for ir commitment to helping the assachusetts Department of cial Services in ensuring that ster children are provided hot, esh, nutritional food while awaiting placement in a safe home," alligan says.

## Recipe for Future Success

The family recipe for success has always been one of serving quality products. Add to that

dynamic leadership, dedicated people, and a passion for high service standards, and one can easily see why the company has such a stronghold in the New England region. Galligan has led Papa Gino's to a position of operating and financial strength over the last four years. This strength will allow accelerated growth of new units to serve more communities with the two premier brands. Galligan predicts, "We plan to open 100 restaurants in New England during the next five years. Our primary focus will remain in New England, but we will undoubtedly expand into new

markets with new franchisees, new concepts, and new products."

## Legacy of Quality, Service, and Value

Papa Gino's Holdings Corporation, Inc. is committed to building upon the legacy of the founders' principles and values to provide high-quality products; attentive service; clean, convenient, attractive restaurants; and a premium value experience for every guest. The company is poised to leverage its position of dominance and leadership throughout New England and beyond.

D'ANGELO WRAPS, INTRODUCED IN 1998, ARE THE HOTTEST NEW SANDWICH CONCEPT IN THE CATEGORY SINCE THE PITA POCKET.

THE SUPER VEGGIE IS ONE OF PAPA GINO'S GOURMET PRIMO PIZZAS.

A N ARBITER OF TASTE FOR GREATER BOSTON'S CULTURAL, culinary, fashion, and social scene, *Boston Magazine* has been bestowing its Best of Boston honors upon individuals and establishments of distinction since 1973. From the best steak tips to the best cigar bar to the best foot-in-mouth statement by a local politician, *Boston Magazine* is the authority on the good

life and culture of Greater Boston. Through its mix of critical reporting, hard-hitting stories, features on services, and reviews of restaurants, movies, and contemporary culture, the magazine has chronicled the major defining moments in the life of Boston, reporting on the people and events that shape the city.

The monthly magazine, headquartered in Boston's Horticultural Hall building, has a circulation of more than 120,000 and an estimated 450,000 readers. *Boston Magazine*'s readers are typically well-educated, upper-income individuals in their

*Boston Magazine*—WHICH HAS A CIR-
CULATION OF MORE THAN 120,000
AND AN ESTIMATED 450,000 READERS—
IS BEST KNOWN FOR ITS ANNUAL BEST
OF BOSTON ISSUE, WHICH IN 1998 IN-
CLUDED MORE THAN 350 CATEGORIES,
RANGING FROM THE SERIOUS TO THE
TONGUE-IN-CHEEK.

40s. About 80 percent of the magazine's issues are sold via subscriptions, with the balance sold on newsstands. *Boston Magazine* employs about 45 people in its editorial, sales, marketing, and circulation departments.

### Covering the Boston Beat

Today's *Boston Magazine* evolved from an earlier publication of the Greater Boston Chamber of Commerce. Since 1971, the magazine has been owned by Philadelphia-based Metrocorp, which also owns *Philadelphia Magazine*. *Boston Magazine*'s advertisers include local and national retailers, fashion and jewelry designers, restaurants and hotels, travel businesses, and high-end automobile makers. The magazine has sales representatives in the New England, New York, Philadelphia, mid-Atlantic, Midwest, West Coast, and Hawaii markets.

Over the years, *Boston Magazine*'s readers have come to expect the magazine to have an opinion, and the magazine has delivered. At its heart, though, the magazine is a serious publication presenting serious journalism. No stranger to controversy, *Boston Magazine* has reported on topics that have spurred debate among its readers and the local community.

The magazine's articles report on city and state politics, legal and business issues, cultural trends, and the city's movers and shakers, both famous and infamous. Committed to publishing investigative reports that look at issues of local concern, *Boston Magazine* was the first to cover the Big Dig construction project's extravagance and budget problems. In addition, the magazine has covered Logan Airport renovations and housing controversies in upscale suburbs such as Weston. The magazine also publishes an

annual Best Places to Live survey, seasonal guides to events and activities, and a Best Doctors in Boston feature, which is widely read and used as a resource by the magazine's readers. Classified advertising and personals are also staples in the publication. Buying guides in the magazine have ranged from how to choose a diamond to how to choose wine.

In addition to its editorial staff's contributions, the magazine features articles written by other local media professionals from television and radio; industry experts, such as defense attorney and Harvard law professor Alan M. Dershowitz; and noted book authors. Former Massachusetts Governor William Weld, for instance, chose *Boston Magazine* to publish an excerpt from his first novel, *Mackerel by Moonlight*, which is set in Boston.

### Part of the Community

In 1997, *Boston Magazine* was named the best city magazine in the country, winning the Gold Medal for General Excellence by the City & Regional Magazine Association (CRMA). In 1998, the magazine was named best regional magazine by *Folio* magazine, winning its Gold Award for general excellence in that category.

*Boston Magazine* is best known for its annual Best of Boston issue, which in 1998 included more than 350 categories, ranging from the serious to the tongue-in-cheek. Winners of the Best of Boston categories frequently tout the awards—which carry a status in Massachusetts and beyond—as part of their own advertising and marketing campaigns.

In conjunction with that issue, *Boston Magazine* for the last 25 years has hosted an annual party for all the Best of Boston winners

IN ADDITION TO ITS EDITORIAL STAFF'S CONTRIBUTIONS, THE MAGAZINE FEATURES ARTICLES WRITTEN BY OTHER LOCAL MEDIA PROFESSIONALS FROM TELEVISION AND RADIO, INDUSTRY EXPERTS, AND NOTED BOOK AUTHORS.

...d their guests. As the magazine ...s expanded its categories in that ...sue over the past decade, the party ...s become an extravaganza with ...ore than 2,000 attendees. The ...lebration also benefits local chari-...es: Each year, *Boston Magazine* ...entifies a charity partner and pro-...des space in the Best of Boston ...sue for that organization to tell its ...ory. In addition, the magazine ...ves the net proceeds from the party ... that charity. The 1998 recipient ...as the Massachusetts Society ...r the Prevention of Cruelty to ...hildren (MSPCC). In addition, ...ery month the magazine contrib-...es substantial space to the *Boston ...agazine* Cares About Boston ...mpaign for local charities, as well ... other public service advertising ...ace.

With recent record increases in ...vertising revenue and newsstand ...adership, *Boston Magazine* has ...oved to expand its brand name ...th some new products. In 1993, the ...blisher launched *New England ...ravel Guide,* published twice an-...ually. In 2000, the guidebook will ... renamed *New England Travel & ...ife* and will be published quarterly. ...ew England Travel & Life* will ...rget a national readership and ...ill focus on the wonderful lifestyle

of New England—America's only equivalent of a European province. In addition, *Boston Magazine*'s *Elegant Wedding* debuted in 1998 and is published twice yearly. Both magazines have been well received by advertisers and newsstand buyers alike. *Boston Magazine* also plans to expand its on-line presence, adding more features and functions to its

Web site, which can be found at www.bostonmagazine.com. Some of these features will augment the magazine's personals advertising.

In the years ahead, *Boston Magazine* will remain an invaluable resource to its readers and will continue fulfilling its mission of reflecting the life of a vibrant, world-class city.

EANE, INC.'S MOTTO—"WE GET IT DONE"—STATES A PRINCIPLE the company has lived by for more than 30 years. The IT is information technology, and Keane's roll-up-your-sleeves, results-driven approach to the development and maintenance of computer software for businesses has propelled the firm into becoming a $1 billion company. ❧ A pioneer in software

services, Keane today is one of the largest and most successful information technology consulting firms. Headquartered in Boston, Keane was cited as the number two company in the 1998 *Boston Globe* Top 100 listing. The public company, which is traded on the American Stock Exchange, was named the best stock performer in the February 1998 *Wall Street Journal*'s Shareholder Scoreboard. In addition, *Computerworld*, in its May 1998 issue, named Keane among the Best Places to Work for an information technology professional.

### A Quick History

John F. Keane, formerly employed at IBM, and Arthur D. Little started the company in 1965 in Hingham. The company quickly became known for Productivity Management, the project management foundation for Keane's application development and outsourcing methodologies.

Keane has grown significantly, completing 17 acquisitions between 1985 and 1998. One of the more strategic acquisitions occurred in June 1998, when Keane acquired Bricker & Associates, which provides business operations improvement consulting services. These services address organizational design, work-flow improvements, and technology strategy. The firm's recommendations help clients achieve 15 to 40 percent revenue increases and reduced costs.

More recently, Keane has acquired Icom Systems Ltd., the parent company of Icom Solutions Ltd.—a privately held, $50 million provider of IT business solutions. Based in Birmingham, England, Icom Systems provided Keane with its first presence in the European marketplace.

Industry analysts have cited Keane's continuity of executive management as one of its strengths. The founder's sons, copresidents Brian T. Keane and John F. Keane

Jr., have helped grow the business, while John F. Keane Sr. continues as the company's chairman, president, and CEO.

### Serving the Customer

Since its beginnings, Keane has been successful at recognizing information technology trends, most recently capitalizing on the year 2000 issue to fuel growth. Keane's effectiveness as a full-service IT partner derives from the company's focus on performance improvement via process and project management disciplines, its world-class capabilities with local delivery, and the ability to plan, build, and manage information technology solutions. Keane's core IT services include Operations Improvement, IT Management Consulting, Application Outsourcing, Application Development, Year 2000 and Migration, and Package Selection and Implementation.

To serve its customers, the company has more than 11,000 employees and 45 branch locations throughout the United States,

TOP: KEANE, INC. UTILIZES ITS SERVICE OFFERINGS, METHODOLOGIES, AND COMPANY SIZE TO "GET IT DONE" FOR CLIENTS.

BOTTOM: THE GREATER BOSTON MANAGEMENT STAFF INCLUDES (FROM LEFT) FRANCIS J. BATES, MANAGING DIRECTOR; KATHY LAPLANTE, OFFICE MANAGER; BRIAN LANCIAULT, STRATEGIC ACCOUNT MANAGER; RICHARD ATKIND, DIRECTOR, EMPLOYEE DEVELOPMENT AND STAFFING; AND JOHN WILKINS (NOT SHOWN), DIRECTOR, SERVICE DELIVERY.

...nada, and the United Kingdom. ...Massachusetts, Keane's Greater ...ston branch, based in Lexington, ...s 400 employees dedicated to ...lving the challenges of their client ...se. This operation services many ...ents, which represent such indus- ...es as retail, financial services, ...nking, publishing, and utilities. ...e leaders in Boston's financial ...rvices industry represent a signifi- ...nt portion of this branch's cus- ...mer base. For these clients, Keane ...ovides a variety of services, includ- ...g performance improvement ...anning, application management ...tsourcing, application develop- ...ent utilizing emerging technolo- ...es, electronic commerce, and data ...arehousing solutions.

...ompany on the Move

...eane moved into the Lexing- ...ton complex after surveying ...ere its clients are located and ...ere its employees live. The 22,000- ...uare-foot facility, which is twice ...e size of the previous location, ...fers Keane the ability to have ...erging technology development ...s, videoconferencing capability, ...f-site development capabilities, ...d an in-house training facility. ...e training curriculum is compe- ...ncy based, concentrating on the ...ur key skill areas required for a ...nsultant to be successful: technol- ...y and methodologies, interper- ...nal, management, and business. ...addition to this competency ...aining, a significant investment ...s been made in compiling an ...tensive library of computer-based ...aining (CBT) modules. "The ...ccessful growth of the Greater ...ston branch, and the company ...a whole, reflects Keane's ability ...rapidly respond to the changing ...eds of our clients and provide a ...sirable work environment for our ...ployees," says Francis J. Bates, ...anaging director.

...Keane's local presence in Boston ...d its offices throughout the ...untry enable the company to be ...ose to its clients, yet leverage the ...pertise of a global organization. ...e company's long-standing focus ...business results has generated ...gnificant repeat business. "Our

services and culture are process driven," says Bates. "We under- stand the advantage of focusing on the processes of developing and managing technology, rather than focusing on the technology itself. As a result, our services solve real business problems and meet impor- tant business requirements."

### Serving the Community

Through the years, Keane, Inc. has remained committed to its core values of respect for the individual, dedication to client success, achievement through team- work, integrity, and the drive to con- tinuously improve. These values also include community responsibility. The scope of Keane's charitable presence extends from branch- initiated efforts—including partici- pation in public television auctions, blood drives, and charity road races— to Keane's support of public educa- tion and a companywide annual charity drive supporting the United Way, Combined Health Appeal, and Earth Share. At the Greater Boston branch, employee-initiated efforts include holiday fund-raising

efforts, food drives, and volunteer- ing time at local shelters and nurs- ing homes.

For the future, the Greater Boston branch has targeted growth in areas that include data warehous- ing, object-oriented development, customer relationship management, electronic commerce, and Web- based development. "Our repeat business exceeds 90 percent each year," says Bates. "That says a lot about how our clients feel about Keane, and confirms that there will be plenty of opportunities for continued growth."

THE TRAINING FACILITY AT THE GREATER BOSTON BRANCH IS UTILIZED TO KEEP THE CONSULTANTS CURRENT ON TECHNOLOGY AND METHODOLO- GIES, INTERPERSONAL, MANAGEMENT, AND BUSINESS COMPETENCIES.

# 1966-1999

| | | | |
|---|---|---|---|
| 1968 | Data General Corporation | 1978 | Lee Kennedy Co., Inc. |
| 1968 | Jung/Brannen Associates, Inc. | 1979 | Boston Scientific Corporation |
| 1968 | Linsco/Private Ledger (LPL Financial Services) | 1980 | CTC Communications |
| 1972 | WCVB-TV | 1980 | Pro Media, Inc. |
| 1974 | Boston Capital Corporation | 1980 | Stratus Computer, Inc. |
| 1977 | Motorola Internet and Networking Group | 1981 | Le Meridien Boston |
| | | 1982 | Massachusetts Convention Center Authority |

**O**NCE THE PROVERBIAL SMOKE-FILLED ROOM OF ONE OF Boston's most important financial institutions, the governor's reception room of the Federal Reserve Bank has a new air of opulence, courtesy of Le Meridien Boston. Since 1981, this once powerful chamber has housed Le Meridien's much acclaimed Julien restaurant. And though the grandeur of the ...storic building remains, today's ...uests are more likely to be a stylish ...vosome out for an elegant evening ...an cigar-smoking barons setting ...scal policy.

**..n Inspired Marriage ...f Old and New**

**M**eridien Hotels & Resorts, a division of London-based ...orte Hotels, has ensured the meticu-...us upkeep of the Renaissance ...evival-style building for nearly ...vo decades. Once a nine-story, ...ranite-and-limestone structure, ...is building has since been trans-...ormed into a 326-room, luxury ...otel that displays fresh elements ...ongside vintage style.

The hotel's Café Fleuri is a won-...erful example of the artful mix of ...d and new. The 180-seat restaurant ...djoins the historic part of the struc-...re and sits beneath a soaring, six-...ory atrium that connects the hotel ... the contemporary One Post Office ...quare tower. Le Meridien has also ...lded three new floors enclosed by ...glass mansard roof at the top of the ...otel. The exquisite design includes ...anted glass walls that offer an ...oundance of light and an expansive ...ew of a bustling downtown Boston. ...ne look reveals that Le Meridien ...ally is at the heart of the city.

While Le Meridien is recognized ...r its architectural beauty, it is per-...aps best known for its wonderful ...pasts. Café Fleuri's Sunday Jazz ...runch is a 10-time winner of ...oston Magazine's Best Sunday ...runch award. The array of sump-...ous culinary creations includes ...âtés, omelets, seafood, freshly ...aked breads, mimosas, and crepes. ...n Saturday afternoons from Sep-...mber through May, Café Fleuri ...osts Le Meridien's award-winning ...hocolate Bar: a decadent array of ...esserts certain to please the most ...dent chocolate lover.

The hotel's widely acclaimed Julien restaurant is named in honor of Boston's first French eatery: Julien's Restorato, which opened in Post Office Square in 1794. Situated beneath gilded, 18-foot, coffered ceilings, Julien is overseen by Executive Chef Alan Raye.

**Where Business and Leisure Travelers Feel at Home**

**F**or business travelers, Le Meridien provides a variety of rooms with a full range of busi-ness amenities. Each room has a two-line phone, voice mail, and a computer hookup, and the hotel staffs a business center with comput-ers and photocopiers, as well as telex, fax, secretarial, and translation ser-vices. In short, guests have instant access to their world so that each day is truly business as usual.

For the weary business traveler, replenishment may be found at Le Club Meridien. Open to all guests on a complimentary basis, the hotel's health club includes a heated swim-ming pool, a whirlpool and sauna, and a full range of exercise equip-ment. Also available are professional trainers, an in-house massage service, and complimentary fruits and beverages.

On weekends, Le Meridien is filled with tourists and families

who enjoy its proximity to some of Boston's most favored and historic attractions, such as the New England Aquarium, the Children's Museum, Faneuil Hall, and the waterfront area. The hotel caters to guests of all ages. This is evident at the children's brunch station, as well as in the children's games, infant toys, cribs, and strollers—all avail-able at the concierge desk.

Le Meridien's reputation as one of Boston's premier luxury hotels is well established. In fact, it's legend-ary. Everyone at the hotel works with a boundless determination for one reason: so guests recognize Le Meridien as the one place where the world really does come together.

CLOCKWISE FROM TOP: FOR BUSINESS TRAVELERS, LE MERIDIEN PROVIDES A VARIETY OF ROOMS WITH A FULL RANGE OF BUSI-NESS AMENITIES.

ONCE A NINE-STORY, GRANITE-AND-LIMESTONE STRUCTURE, THE HISTORIC FEDERAL RESERVE BANK BUILDING HAS SINCE BEEN TRANSFORMED INTO A 326-ROOM, LUXURY HOTEL THAT DIS-PLAYS FRESH ELEMENTS ALONGSIDE VINTAGE STYLE.

THE HOTEL'S WIDELY ACCLAIMED JULIEN RESTAURANT IS NAMED IN HONOR OF BOSTON'S FIRST FRENCH EATERY: JULIEN'S RESTORATO, WHICH OPENED IN POST OFFICE SQUARE IN 1794.

# Linsco/Private Ledger (LPL Financial Services)

L INSCO/PRIVATE LEDGER (LPL FINANCIAL SERVICES) BELIEVES I the value of independent, unbiased, no-strings-attached financi advice. Through a national network of more than 2,900 finan cial advisers located in 1,500 locally owned and operated branc offices in all 50 states and Puerto Rico, LPL provides its client with objective advice and access to investments from many of th

nation's leading money management companies. At year-end 1997, LPL advisers had invested or were managing nearly $28 billion in client assets. LPL's clients are independent financial advisers, financial institutions, insurance companies, certified public accountants, and registered investment advisers.

Two key points set LPL representatives apart. First, LPL Financial Services has deliberately chosen not to offer proprietary products, and that choice preserves the integrity of investment advice given by LPL representatives. Rather than creating and marketing its own investment products, LPL concentrates on providing service to its financial advisers, who are free to recommend investments that are best suited to their clients' risk tolerance and investment objectives.

Second, LPL representatives are business owners in the communi-

ties they serve, and this ownership stake creates a strong link between individual LPL representatives and their clients. LPL's commitment to providing top-notch customer service to its financial representatives is the cornerstone of the company's foundation.

## A Boston Legacy

L PL has dual corporate headquarters, located in the heart of Boston's financial district and in San Diego's emerging technology center. These offices are staffed with more than 350 employees who service the business of all LPL financial advisers. In the Greater Boston area, there are more than 150 LPL financial advisers. "Boston is the perfect home for LPL: The well-educated city is driven by technology and research, and is the mutual fund capital of the nation," says Todd Robinson, LPL chairman and CEO.

The company has a solid histor of having served independent representatives for 30 years. Linsco was established in 1968 in Boston, and Private Ledger began operations in 1973 in San Diego. Both firms were founded on the basic principle that local branch ownership by financial professionals enables them to serve their clients more efficiently, while allocating their resources more effectively. Local ownership, both firms found results in a higher level of profitability and, more important, satisfaction to the representative.

Robinson bought Linsco in 198 and merged it with Private Ledger in 1989. By combining the forces o these two enterprises, LPL was abl to attain the critical mass to develo new programs and services and to expand the existing technology. Wit an experienced management team in place, the firm began building a

"BOSTON IS THE PERFECT HOME FOR LPL: THE WELL-EDUCATED CITY IS DRIVEN BY TECHNOLOGY AND RESEARCH, AND IS THE MUTUAL FUND CAPITAL OF THE NATION," SAYS TODD A. ROBINSON, LPL CHAIRMAN AND CEO (LEFT).

UNDER THE LEADERSHIP OF EXECUTIVES SUCH AS DAVID H. BUTTERFIELD, PRESIDENT AND COO, LPL HAS ATTAINED THE CRITICAL MASS TO DEVELOP NEW PROGRAMS AND SERVICES, AND EXPAND EXISTING TECHNOLOGY (RIGHT).

rong infrastructure to better serve representatives. The company's nique position—independent from ny product provider—enabled LPL focus on delivering unbiased search, cutting-edge technology, d operational support to its financial representatives.

Since the merger, the firm has corded nine successive years of cord earnings and revenues. In 97, LPL's total revenues of $354 illion made it the largest independent financial services firm in e nation for the third consecutive ar, according to *Financial Planning* agazine's June 1998 broker/dealer rvey.

Robinson has also been recognized for his leadership. In 1997, he as elected chairman of the board governors of NASD Regulation, c., the front-line regulator of the ation's 5,500 broker/dealers and 6,000 registered representatives. obinson played a key role in eveloping the industry's now-andatory continuing education quirements. LPL's continuing ducation program for its represen-tives received the NASD's "best actices" recognition.

## erving Representatives' Needs

oday, LPL's wide range of services includes financial lanning, advisory services, research, formation technology, fee-based set management, trading, portfo-o analysis, insurance, long-term are, tax-free investing, and retire-ent planning. Products offered by PL include mutual funds, fixed d variable annuities, insurance, ocks, and bonds. In 1997, LPL ad $2.8 billion in sales in mutual nds, and $1.5 billion in variable nnuities. More than 1 million ansactions were exectued through PL in 1997.

The Strategic Asset Management AM) program, launched in 1991, the flagship of LPL's Advisory ervices department. SAM offers vestors access to 2,800 actively anaged no-load/load-waived utual funds, as well as individual ocks and bonds. SAM capitalizes n a building trend toward provid-g investors with fee-based, rather

than commission-based, investment advice and portfolio management. The SAM program currently has nearly $9 billion in assets under management. The benefit for in-vestors is clear: the ability to have a portfolio structured within a stra-tegic asset allocation framework, ongoing advice, and quarterly per-formance statements. Clients pay an annual fee based on the account's overall value.

LPL also has developed desktop technology for its financial planners, including a contact and portfolio management system, account re-balancing, and financial planning software, as well as establishing a presence on the World Wide Web.

The company has supported the Boston community through its annual Kids Week charity event.

Since 1993, LPL has been host-ing more than 500 children and sponsors from the Big Brother Association of Boston for dinner and a Red Sox game at Fenway Park. The company hosts a similar event at the San Diego Padres ball-park. "We think Kids Week is an excellent means for LPL to give something back to the com-munity we live and work in," says Robinson.

In the years ahead, Robinson says LPL will continue to maintain its independence from investment products while focusing on tech-nological initiatives and objective research that provide LPL financial advisers with more efficiency in the management of their clients' investment portfolios, and of their own daily operations.

CVB-TV, New England's Channel 5, is the essence of what a local television station can mean to a community. Since its on-air debut on March 19, 1972, WCVB—today a division of Hearst-Argyle Television, Inc.—has attracted more viewers than any other area station to its comprehensive and insightful news; thorough coverage of special events;

thought-provoking, original programming; and broad range of entertainment offerings. Few stations in the country have made as great a contribution to a community's life, culture, and charity. And no station in America has been honored with so many of broadcasting's top awards.

Channel 5 is, indeed, family to New England—Natalie, Chet, Dick, Mike, Mary, and Peter are the first names of Boston television. Behind them are the talented and respected reporters, producers, and editors of NewsCenter 5 and the nightly news-magazine *Chronicle;* the staff of the urban magazine *CityLine;* and the news analysts of the Sunday panel show *Five on 5*. Channel 5's extended family includes the ABC network with its *World News Tonight with Peter Jennings, 20/20, Good Morning America*, and *Nightline*, and the thousands of people engaged in presenting one of the country's most popular prime-time TV schedules.

## The Most-Watched News

The most-watched news in New England, NewsCenter 5 presents six separate newscasts each day: the *EyeOpener* from 5 to 7 a.m., the *Midday* from noon to 12:30 p.m., three complete half-hour newscasts between 5 and 6:30 p.m., and *NewsCenter 5 Tonight* from 11 to 11:35 p.m. Principal news anchors are husband-and-wife team Chet Curtis and Natalie Jacobson, both of whom have been with the station since its founding. Over the years, Jacobson and Curtis have hosted live coverage of virtually every major event broadcast by Channel 5, including elections, presidential and papal visits, and start-to-finish coverage of the annual Boston Marathon. Their top-rated anchor team is complemented by chief meteorologist Dick Albert, one of Boston television's most popular personalities, and acclaimed sports anchor Mike Lynch.

NewsCenter 5 has been honored with the most prestigious awards in

broadcasting. In 1998, the station captured the highest honor in the esteemed Gabriel Awards competition by being named Television Station of the Year. Also in 1998, NewsCenter 5 was bestowed the nationally coveted Edward R. Murrow Award for Overall Excellence by the Radio and Television News Directors Association.

## Leading the Way in Local Programming

WCVB has consistently produced and broadcast more local programming than virtually any other station in the country, in committing as much as 25 percent of its airtime to local productions over its history. A significant national milestone in local programming was the debut of WCVB's *Chronicle* in January 1982. Still going strong in its 7:30 to 8 p.m. time slot as the only locally produced nightly news magazine of its size and scope in the country, *Chronicle*, cohosted

NewsCenter 5 provides Boston with the most comprehensive local news. (Large photo, from left) Meteorologist Dick Albert joins the principal anchor team of Natalie Jacobson and Chet Curtis, along with SportsCenter 5's Mike Lynch every weeknight for three comprehensive newscasts. (Top inset) Heather Kahn and Brian Leary focus on the events of the day at 5:30 p.m. (Bottom inset) Peter Mehegan and Mary Richardson present intriguing features and special reports every night at 7:30 p.m. on *Chronicle*.

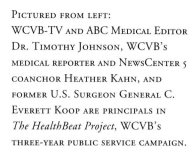

y respected broadcast journalists Mary Richardson and Peter Mehegan, resents a mix of fast-breaking ocal, national, and international tories, as well as informative feature reports on the people, places, nd events of New England and he world.

Channel 5 was one of the first nd only stations to produce comprehensive programming in the reas of law and health, with Harvard aw School professor Arthur Miller nd Dr. Timothy Johnson, who oday continue their work with WCVB while also serving the ABC network in their specialties.

In 1981, Channel 5 produced a made-for-television film, *Summer Solstice* starring Henry Fonda, which ired on the ABC television network, and in 1989, WCVB became he only local station to produce a program for the ABC series *Afterschool Specials* with "The Cheats."

## Unprecedented Community Service

The station's critically acclaimed public service campaigns have lso received national recognition. *Family Works!*, a celebration of amily values, aired in 120 markets nd reached 75 percent of the ountry. *The HealthBeat Project*, a hree-year public service campaign ledicated to improving the health nd physical well-being of viewers, s currently being aired on the tation with the participation of ormer Surgeon General C. Everett Koop. It includes numerous original

prime-time specials, news series, and public service announcements. Other campaigns have included the ongoing *Success by 6*, which is partnered through the United Way of Massachusetts Bay and is aimed at helping the area's youngest children, and *A World of Difference*, a major anti-prejudice effort sponsored with the Anti-Defamation League (ADL). *A World of Difference* was nationally syndicated by the ADL and received praise from the White House, among many other groups.

WCVB produces dozens of specials every year, including prime-time and weekend programming. The station has fostered a unique partnership with the Boston Symphony Orchestra and Boston Pops, producing, among other programs, the annual *Salute to Symphony* and the Fourth of July outdoor extravaganza *Pops! Goes the Fourth*, nationally broadcast by the A&E network. The station also teams with A&E for a national simulcast

of the perennial holiday favorite *Holiday at Pops*, and has partnered with the History Channel on two one-hour documentaries titled *The Hidden History of Boston.*

With annual on-air telethons, Channel 5 raises millions of dollars for a variety of charities, including the Muscular Dystrophy Association, United Cerebral Palsy, and Boston's Genesis Fund, to benefit children born with physical challenges. The station has lent on-air support to countless other philanthropies, such as the United Way, Boston Public Library, Massachusetts Coalition for the Homeless, Salvation Army, and American Heart Association.

## Ushering in New Technology

WCVB has a proud past, but it also has an exciting future. With new digital hardware, WCVB was the first New England station to transmit HDTV (high definition television). Channel 5's on-line site (www.wcvb.com)—the first of any TV station's to report more than 1 million hits in a single week—features streamed video of daily newscasts and an interactive weather site for children, among other features.

So, whether on-line or on-air, to New Englanders everywhere, television is best defined by what WCVB does—in its news coverage, local programming, and community service. As the 21st century approaches, WCVB will be there for New England and its people, as a trusted family member, still innovating, still serving—still the one to watch.

# B

**B**OSTON CAPITAL CORPORATION HAS FLOURISHED UNDER TH simple philosophy of "doing well by doing good." This full integrated and diversified real estate firm maintains a focus o producing high-quality, affordable housing, providing homes fo many of America's elderly, disabled, and families of modes means. From a two-man partnership, the company has grow

FROM A TWO-MAN PARTNERSHIP BE-
TWEEN HERBERT F. COLLINS (TOP LEFT)
AND JOHN P. MANNING, BOSTON
CAPITAL CORPORATION HAS GROWN TO
INCLUDE MORE THAN 200 EMPLOYEES
IN BOSTON AND AROUND THE COUN-
TRY, BECOMING THE FIFTH-LARGEST
OWNER OF MULTIFAMILY HOUSING IN
THE UNITED STATES, WITH MORE THAN
2,000 PROPERTIES IN 48 STATES.

BOSTON CAPITAL INSTITUTIONAL
ADVISORS (BCIA) HAS PROVIDED
MEZZANINE AND EQUITY FINANCING
FOR PROPERTIES SUCH AS ONE BRATTLE
SQUARE IN CAMBRIDGE.

to include more than 200 employees in Boston and around the country, becoming the fifth-largest owner of multifamily housing in the United States, with more than 2,000 properties in 48 states.

The company has certainly come a long way from its humble beginnings. In 1974, Herbert F. Collins, chairman, and John P. Manning, president and CEO, formed Boston Capital. "Jack and I had a vision back then that at some point in time, we'd become a holding company with a lot of subcomponents," notes Collins, "and that vision has evolved into reality." Today, Boston Capital is a parent organization with five affiliates: Boston Capital Asset Management; Boston Capital Services; Boston Capital Partners; Boston Capital Institutional Advisors; and Boston Capital Housing. The company has a real estate portfolio in excess of $6 billion. Working

under one roof, these affiliates share their individual expertise to make Boston Capital a leader in the real estate finance industry.

### Providing Affordable Housing

In 1986, Collins and Manning served as a resource for Congress in devising the Low Income Housing Tax Credit program, which aimed to bolster private investment in the

development of affordable housing Through the program, developers can build housing at a reasonable profit; tenants can enjoy quality, affordable apartment units; and investors are able to contribute to the well-being of their communities while reducing their federal taxes. This program has since accounted for more than 900,000 new units of affordable housing nationwide, of which 72,000 are owned by Boston Capital.

Today, affordable housing differs from conventional apartment buildings only in the financing. Private investment through the tax credit program allows the properties to maintain relatively low mortgage financing, which results in lower, affordable rents. Boston Capital ha provided capital for the development of primarily smaller, garden-style apartment complexes in rural, suburban, and metropolitan areas.

### Creating Portfolios

Nationally recognized as a leading sponsor of tax credit funds, Boston Capital creates diversified property portfolios for individual and institutional investors, who then receive annual tax credits. About 60,000 individuals and corporations have invested more than $1.6 billion in order to receive

e reliability of a higher-yielding, ter-tax, fixed-income investment.

In 1993, when Congress made e Tax Credit Program a permaent part of the Internal Revenue ode, corporate investors, includg many Fortune 500 companies, came substantial investors in oston Capital's tax credit funds. long with larger funds to accomodate their sizable investments, ese corporations needed more phisticated information to satisfy eir boards of directors and stockolders. In response to their needs, oston Capital Asset Management veloped a proprietary informaon management system. The firm rrently tracks more than 54,000 parate pieces of information perining to 2,000 properties in 48 ates, making it one of the larger set management companies in the untry.

Although most of the properties cluded in the tax credit funds are ew construction, Boston Capital ousing uses the company's experse to finance the rehabilitation of d HUD housing projects. Under is program, Boston Capital aids the restoration of these apartents, preserving them as affordle units through tax credit nancing.

In keeping with its goal to be full service real estate investment m, Boston Capital Institutional dvisors (BCIA) concentrates on ore conventional real estate investments, such as single-tenant et-leased office properties, mezzane debt on commercial properes, and investing on behalf of reign institutional clients. BCIA as recently raised more than $285 illion for the acquisition of single-nant net-leased office properties, d provided mezzanine and equity nancing for properties such as ne Brattle Square in Cambridge. CIA's rapidly growing portfolio xceeds $400 million and 8 million uare feet of commercial property.

## oston Capital Foundation

A s an expression of commitment to the community, ollins and Manning created the oston Capital Foundation in 1995.

Since its inception, the foundation has contributed in excess of $400,000 to charities in Boston and around the country, including YouthBuild USA; the Boston Partners in Education's Read Boston program; the Ron Burton Training Village; and the John F. Kennedy Library Foundation's Distinguished Visitors Program. In addition to direct contributions, Boston Capital has also utilized its expertise in real estate finance to assist a number of charitable organizations. In 1990, for example, Boston Capital provided the equity financing for the reha-

bilitation of a number of housing facilities administered by the Pine Street Inn, an organization dedicated to serving the needs of Boston's homeless men and women.

With hopes of continued success and growth, Boston Capital Corporation is poised to provide the highest level of service and innovation to the rapidly changing real estate industry. Boston Capital remains committed to using its expertise to make significant contributions to society, continuing to live by its philosophy of "doing well by doing good."

BOSTON CAPITAL HAS PROVIDED CAPITAL FOR THE DEVELOPMENT OF PRIMARILY SMALLER, GARDEN-STYLE APARTMENT COMPLEXES IN RURAL, SUBURBAN, AND METROPOLITAN AREAS.

THE WAY PEOPLE COMMUNICATE AND CONDUCT BUSINESS HA changed dramatically over the course of the 1990s, thanks to the Internet; the emergence of digital networks; the convergence of voice, video, and data; and the linkage between communication and computing. Motorola's Internet and Networking Group (ING), headquartered in Mansfield, has positioned itself at the forefront of this transformation in the methods by which people and organizations connect in a world of converging communications. Motorola ING pulls together critical businesses, technologies, and skill sets in the areas of networking, Internet access, software connectivity, and content services.

### Global Reach, Local Roots

Motorola ING is a division of Schaumburg, Illinois-based Motorola Inc., which first established a presence in Massachusetts in 1977 with the acquisition of Codex Corp. (founded in 1962), a leading supplier of communications equipment and services. Motorola Inc.—which had sales totaling $29.8 billion in 1997—maintains sales, service, and manufacturing facilities throughout the world; conducts business on six continents; and employs more than 130,000 people worldwide.

Motorola, Inc. is a global leader in software-energized wireless communications, semiconductors, and advanced electronic systems and services. Motorola creates cellular telephones, two-way radios, and paging, data, and satellite communications systems. The company's embedded semiconductors are essential digital building blocks for consumer networking and computing, transportation, and wireless communications markets. Motorola, Inc.'s other businesses include automotive electronics, components, computing, and energy products.

In July 1998, Motorola, Inc. formed Motorola Communications Enterprise (CE), and today, Motorola ING is part of the CE division. With 1,250 employees in Massachusetts, Motorola ING comprises four business areas: corporate networking (networking products and services for the enterprise); broadband communications (high-speed Internet access and telephony for the home); wireless content service (information services for wireless devices); and platform software (operating systems, clients, and servers for wireless devices). The first two of these business divisions are based in Massachusetts.

### Cyber Surfing

Within ING, the Multimedia Group develops, manufactures, and markets systems for the convergence of voice, data, and video communications services over advanced broadband multimedia platforms. Motorola's Multimedia Group holds 60 percent of the cable modem market share, and had 1998 revenues of about $100 million. The group's CableComm technology includes the CyberSURFR® cable modem, Cable Router, Cable Access unit, Cable Control Frame, and operations and maintenance center. Throughout 1997 and 1998, Motorola shipped 300,000 cable modems.

The CyberSURFR cable modem connects a subscriber's personal computer or other TCP/IP (transmission control protocol/Internet protocol) addressable device to a hybrid fiber/coaxial (HFC) system. The cable data system is specifically designed for high-speed communications through on-line services, Internet access, telecommuting, and other emerging services for home and business PC users. Customers for these cable modem systems include the top five cable operators in the United States: TCI, Time Warner, Cox, Comcast, and MediaOne. In addition, Motorola's CyberSURFR cable modem was used for the first-ever national interactive gaming tournament hosted by Comcast@Home.

International customers for the company include Optus and Telstra in Australia, France Telecom

IN ADDITION TO ITS CABLE DATA AND NETWORKING PRODUCTS, MOTOROLA'S MASSACHUSETTS FACILITY ALSO PROVIDES ON-LINE NETWORK MANAGEMENT SERVICES TO COMPANIES AROUND THE WORLD.

MOTOROLA'S AUTOMATED HIGH-SPEED PRODUCTION LINES ASSEMBLE PRODUCTS THAT LINK HOMES AND BUSINESSES TO THE INFORMATION SUPERHIGHWAY (TOP).

BESIDES DESIGNING AND BUILDING AWARD-WINNING PRODUCTS, MOTOROLA SUPPORTS COMMUNITY ACTIVITIES, SUCH AS JUNIOR ACHIEVEMENT (BOTTOM).

V Cable Bogota in Columbia, V Cable Ecuador in Quito, and omtech in Guatemala City. With ptus, Motorola's Multimedia roup has the world's largest cable lephony system.

In addition to the product lines, e Multimedia Group's CyberSeed vestments program supports e development of emerging com- anies that will bring broadband cess and enabling devices to ansport networks, as well as com- anies that will benefit from high- eed data access to homes and usinesses. The new CyberSeed enture Program was created to imulate the growth of companies at provide customers with revenue- nerating development tools, in- ractive services, and content. hrough this support, the program ill maximize the potential of roadband networks as they are eployed worldwide.

**eading the Industry**

Another key group within ING is the Multiservice etworks Division (MND), which ables businesses and other orga- izations to profit from the power f multimedia communications. IND develops, manufactures, d markets products that tie an ganization's computers together to networks, whether those com-

puters are located on a single cam- pus or in many locations around the globe. More significantly, these networking devices enable compa- nies to save money by carrying data, image, sound, and motion over a single communications network.

From there, the next step has been to enable businesses to lever- age the Internet and its relations (intranets and extranets) to build competitive advantages. For example, Motorola has been a pioneer and continuing leader in developing technology that enables voice tele- phone calls over the Internet. Voice over the Internet Protocol (VoIP) enables, for example, someone browsing through an on-line cata- log to call the retailer directly over the Internet. Not surprising for a company that also pioneered voice over the frame relay network. By breaking voice messages into small components called packets, Motorola enabled these calls to be sent over a cost-effective network called frame relay that once could only carry data. Now Motorola Vanguard® networking products and transmis- sion devices are enabling companies around the world to save money while growing their business by building high-performance informa- tion networks that give them the technological edge to win the future.

**Connecting with the Community**

Motorola ING and its em- ployees have been involved in numerous educational activities, such as providing scholarships and Internet connectivity equipment to local schools and volunteering time for fund-raisers and other events. The company has also do- nated time and money to social and human service organizations in the area, including United Way and the New England Home for Little Wanderers.

With its long-standing com- mitment to technology leadership and quality, Motorola ING is now leveraging the company's history and expertise to pioneer the next generation of telecommunications and networking.

# Lee Kennedy Co., Inc.

**W**HEN PATRONS OF THE NEWLY RENOVATED BOSTON PUBLI Library's McKim Building enter the elegant and masterfu interiors of this national historic landmark, they will view the handicraft of Lee Kennedy Co., Inc. The Boston-base general contractor was chosen by the City of Boston fo this important project because of its reputation fo sensitive restoration work and its appreciation of historic architecture.

The importance of preserving architectural landmarks stems from the founder's roots. Lee M. Kennedy, chairman and CEO, was introduced to architecture at an early age. Kennedy worked in his family's office, the nationally recognized firm of Maginnis Walsh & Kennedy, which was involved in the late 1930s interior renovation of Trinity Church in the Back Bay; the National Shrine of the Immaculate Conception in Washington, D.C.; and Baltimore's Cathedral of Mary Our Queen. After working for the firm as an architectural draftsman, Kennedy left to work in the construction field, learning the business by working as a laborer, ironworker, and crane operator. Kennedy then joined a specialty subcontracting

firm and developed total design-build data processing facilities for clients in New England.

Kennedy founded Lee Kennedy Co. in 1978. Since then, the company has expanded to provide a wide range of services, including preconstruction, construction management, and general contracting services. The company has grown to employ 37 in-house and approximately 100 regular field personnel. Projects include interior renovations, new construction, additions, and historic restorations for the commercial, retail, and institutional markets.

Many Kennedy projects have involved the challenging restoration and reconstruction of historically important buildings. The majority of construction work for the Boston Public Library's McKim Building, Harvard University's Sanders Theater, the New England Genealogical Society, and the New England College of Optometry Library was done by hand, due to the delicate nature of the surrounding materials and because the buildings had to remain open throughout construction.

Institutional experience includes the fast-track design-build addition and renovation to Northeastern University's Student Center; a new,

95,000-square-foot athletic complex for Harvard University that includes six tennis courts and 16 squash courts; a new radio station, classrooms, and cafés for Emerson College; Trim Dining Hall and Coleman Hall Dormitory at Babson College; a new hockey arena and gymnasium for Milton Academy; and a new, six-building campus for a special needs school on Cape Cod.

Successful retail construction is ongoing for Lee Kennedy Co. Projects range from the new, 40,000-square-foot CompUSA superstore on Massachusetts Avenue to the award-winning Willowbee & Kent Travel Company on Boylston Street, as well as many area restaurants. In addition, Lee Kennedy Co. was the general contractor for the interior build-out of the new FleetCenter, home to the Bruins and Celtics.

Lee Kennedy Co. has been the general contractor for many clients and architects throughout New England who require quality construction within critical deadlines. Lee Kennedy Co. has been the choice of many commercial tenant such as New England Financial, Liberty Mutual, John Hancock, Bronner Slosberg Humphrey,

BOSTON PUBLIC LIBRARY'S BATES HALL FEATURES THE LARGEST BARREL-VAULTED CEILING IN NORTH AMERICA. THE CEILING, WHICH SPANS 218 FEET, WAS RESTORED COMPLETELY BY HAND UNDER THE MANAGEMENT OF LEE KENNEDY CO., INC. (TOP).

LEE KENNEDY BUILT A STEEL STAIR TO CONNECT THE 18TH AND 19TH FLOORS OF THIS PUBLIC RELATIONS FIRM IN THE PRUDENTIAL TOWER. THE PROJECT ENCOMPASSED EIGHT FLOORS (BOTTOM).

MARCO LORENZETTI

ankBoston, Investors Bank & Trust, and Massachusetts Financial Services.

Most recently, Lee Kennedy Co. has been awarded the multimillion-dollar renovation and restoration of the historic Widener Library at Harvard University, the new International Cargo Port at South Boston's Marine Industrial Park, and a 1,000-car parking garage for Northeastern University.

Under the leadership of Kennedy and President Robert J. McCluskey, the company is actively involved in industry professional groups and charitable endeavors. McCluskey started his career as a field superintendent for Lee Kennedy Co. 18 years ago. He worked for a time with other contractors and, in 1994, Kennedy offered the presidency and partnership to his longtime friend. Since that time, McCluskey has taken the company to a position of leadership in the New England region. "I see Bob as a mentor for my three children, who are all part of the company," says Kennedy, who adds that continuing the com-

pany's family tradition is a "tremendous source of pride to me." Lee Michael, who has been with the firm for 18 years, is vice president of administration; Gene has been with the firm nine years and is project manager; and Shaila, who has been with the firm eight years, is director of marketing. "They learned the business the way I did: by working in the field," says Kennedy.

McCluskey is past president of the New England Construction Users Council and past director of the Construction Industry Liaison Group. Kennedy serves on the board of directors for the Franciscan Children's Hospital and Rehabilitation Center, the Colonel Daniel Marr Boys and Girls Club, the South Boston Harbor Academy Charter School, the BankBoston Development Company, and Atlantic Data Services.

The company is committed to helping the community, providing construction services pro bono for several nonprofit organizations. "If we're financially able, it's important to replenish parts of the community

that need help," says Kennedy. The firm's charitable work includes construction of Bridge Over Troubled Waters; renovations to the Colonel Daniel Marr Boys and Girls Club; construction management services overseeing renovations to the Mother Theresa House; and construction of the South Boston Neighborhood House, the new South Boston Harbor Academy Charter School, and the new Paul R. McLaughlin Teen Center in Dorchester, Massachusetts.

From the largest commercial corporation to the smallest nonprofit community organization, each Kennedy project is characterized by quality. The Kennedy formula for both new construction and outstanding restoration and renovation combines an intimate knowledge of architecture, a deep appreciation of the architectural heritage of Boston and New England, and the skills of a professional group of tradesmen and -women, with the ability to manage demanding construction projects.

CLOCKWISE FROM TOP:
A UNIQUE TRAVEL SHOP COMPLETED BY LEE KENNEDY IN ONLY NINE WEEKS INCLUDES A CUSTOM-CRAFTED SPIRAL STAIRCASE, HANDICAPPED LIFT, THEATRICAL LIGHTING, AND STATE-OF-THE-ART TECHNOLOGY.

A NEW ATHLETIC COMPLEX BUILT BY THE FIRM HOUSES AN ICE RINK, BASKETBALL COURTS, A WEIGHT TRAINING FACILITY, AND ATHLETIC DEPARTMENT OFFICES.

LEE KENNEDY COMPLETED A NEW PHYSICAL THERAPY CLINIC LOCATED ON THE FIRST FLOOR OF NORTHEASTERN UNIVERSITY'S MARINO RECREATION CENTER.

UIDED BY A MISSION THAT HAS NOT CHANGED IN MORE THAN 2 years, Boston Scientific Corporation is committed to developir the technology of minimally invasive medicine and therapy t improve patient outcomes and reduce health care costs. Th. thinking has made the company a leader in the development an manufacture of products that make minimally invasive therap

possible. Beginning with the steerable catheter in 1969, a device that enabled physicians to navigate the body's vasculature, Boston Scientific's product offerings now include more than 16,000 items in over 60 categories. Each medical device enables physicians to access, study, and treat patients through tiny openings in the body that are often smaller than the tip of a pencil. These products allow physicians to intervene earlier and more precisely, with less risk, less trauma, and reduced hospital stays for patients. By delivering more efficient diagnoses and treatments through minimally invasive therapies, health care providers are able to reduce procedural costs.

Today, Natick-based Boston Scientific Corporation is the larg-

est medical device company in the world dedicated to minimally invasive therapy, with six operating divisions, 14,000 employees worldwide, and 10 manufacturing and technology centers around the globe. Boston Scientific has direct-sales operations in more than 50 countries and distributorships in 80, along with five major distribution centers in Quincy, Massachusetts; Beek, Netherlands; Singapore; Buenos Aires; and Tokyo. Sales for the company in 1997 totaled $1.87 billion, a 21 percent increase from the previous year.

Boston Scientific's symbol is a ship in a balloon, a medical variation on the ship in the bottle. It represents the challenging task of diagnosing and treating damaged

organs or vessels through tiny openings from a remote location—the essence of interventional or minimally invasive procedures.

### Pioneers in Less Invasive Medicine

Boston Scientific's history bega in the late 1960s, when the company's director, cofounder, anc chairman, John Abele, acquired ar equity interest in Medi-tech, Inc., a Watertown, Massachusetts-base development company. Medi-tech' initial products—a family of steerab catheters—were used in some of the first less invasive procedures performed.

In 1979, Abele joined Peter Nicholas, the company's director, cofounder, CEO, and board chair

NATICK-BASED BOSTON SCIENTIFIC CORPORATION IS THE LARGEST MEDICAL DEVICE COMPANY IN THE WORLD DEDICATED TO MINIMALLY INVASIVE THERAPY.

man, to form Boston Scientific Corporation for the purpose of acquiring Medi-tech, Inc. The acquisition began a period of focused marketing efforts, new product development, and organizational growth. In 1992, the company completed its initial public offering, and today its stock is traded on the New York Stock Exchange under the symbol BSX.

## Developing New Markets

Boston Scientific's innovative technology is developed through consultations and collaborations with leading physicians. One of the initial partnerships was with Joachim Burhenne, a pioneer in less invasive medical procedures. Since the early 1970s, Burhenne has been a partner with Medi-tech, where he developed a technique for nonoperative removal of retained gallstones. This new procedure, which required the use of a steerable catheter, eliminated the need for surgery.

Already the owner of more than 1,000 patents, Boston Scientific is continuing to expand its technolo-gies and product offerings. The company recently received FDA approval to sell three coronary stents in the United States. Metallic stents are implantable devices that act as scaffolds to hold open a particular structure, such as a blood vessel that is obstructed by disease. Stents improve patient outcomes and offer new options for the treatment and management of cardio-vascular, vascular, and nonvascular diseases.

Other core technologies Boston Scientific is developing include catheter-based ultrasound imaging systems, which provide precise diagnostic information to improve the ability of physicians to select appropriate therapy and assess their interventions. The technology has the potential to revolutionize the management of cardiovascular disease and cancer therapy. The company is also developing technologies for localized drug delivery that will allow direct drug application at the disease site. This technology may improve the long-term success rates of angioplasty and other vascular interventions, as well as unmask new treatment options.

Boston Scientific has grown through mergers, alliances, and acquisitions with companies whose technologies and products complement or enhance the firm's portfolio for the total treatment of particular disease states. Most recently, Boston Scientific acquired Schneider Worldwide, a member of the Medical Technology Group of Pfizer, Inc. and a leader in angioplasty treatment, and CardioGene Therapeutics, Inc., a development-state enterprise that focuses on the application of gene therapy for treatment of cardiovascular diseases.

Through its continued innovation, its commitment to providing physicians with the right products for patients, and the building of a world-class organization, Boston Scientific remains committed to its mission: To improve patient care and health care delivery through the development and advocacy of less invasive medical devices and procedures.

BOSTON SCIENTIFIC'S WORLD-CLASS MANUFACTURING STRENGTHENS THE COMPANY'S COMMITMENT TO DELIVERING PRODUCTS OF SUPERIOR QUALITY.

THE DEREGULATION OF THE TELECOMMUNICATIONS INDUSTRY has created unprecedented options for small and medium-sized businesses. In today's wired world—where the choices made one day can make or break a business the next—it pays to have the right connections. CTC Communications, a Waltham-based corporation, has been guiding businesses through the

CLOCKWISE FROM TOP RIGHT: SUPERIOR CUSTOMER SERVICE—DEMONSTRATED BY A 95 PERCENT CUSTOMER RETENTION RATE—IS THE FOUNDATION OF CTC COMMUNICATIONS' SUCCESS.

THE CTC INFORMATION SYSTEM GIVES CUSTOMER SERVICE REPRESENTATIVES QUICK ACCESS TO ALL THE INFORMATION THEY NEED, ENSURING RESPONSIVE, EFFICIENT SERVICE.

CTC'S EXPANSION PLANS INCLUDE BUILDING A CARRIER-GRADE NETWORK WITH HUBS IN NEW YORK, NEW JERSEY, AND NEW ENGLAND.

telecommunications revolution since 1980.

CTC is an integrated communications provider (ICP), offering a full range of telecommunications services: local and long distance, Internet access, high-speed data networking, and complete customer support. With 25 strategically located branch offices, CTC is poised to become a leading telecommunications provider throughout the Northeast corridor—a fact not lost on industry analysts. The company has been recognized by *Forbes* as one of the nation's Top 200

Small Businesses, and by *Business Week* as one of 1997's hot growth companies. Locally, CTC has made the *Boston Globe*'s Top 100 Public Companies list, as well as the *Boston Herald*'s Top 97 in '97 list.

## Premier Products and Premier Service

Unlike typical local and long-distance service providers, CTC analyzes each client's current telecommunications needs and usage, then tailors a cost-saving plan that may include local exchange services, internal telephone systems,

800 services, discount calling services, and calling card programs. The company provides comprehensive administrative support at every stage, from pricing and ordering through implementation and billing.

For high-speed data networking, CTC offers ISDN (integrated services digital network), DDS (digital data services), T-1, frame relay, and other broadband applications. For Internet access, clients can choose from a range of direct connection options, from standard 56K access to high-speed fractional T-3 lines, plus host services, network security consultations, and dial-up access to corporate intranets.

Having the industry's best products and pricing is only part of the story. CTC acts as a network consultant and communications partner, keeping an eye on the industry so that busy entrepreneurs can focus on core activities. With an extensive array of technological, management, and information tools, CTC works with clients to create a seamless communications network. With more than 10,000 business clients, hundreds of thousands of customer service orders processed, and thousands of networks designed and implemented, CTC boasts a 95 percent customer retention rate—a figure unmatched in the industry.

One of the tools that makes the firm's high level of customer satisfaction possible is the CTC Information System. The system integrates all of the company's critical functions: marketing, customer care, provisioning, billing, and financial processes. Information is shared between functions and is available to branch offices in real time, allowing for accurate,

ficient communication and service delivery.

Here's how it works: The Account Management System, one component of CTC's Information System, stores every customer's transaction history and account profile. It feeds the Customized Sales System, a database that helps sales personnel monitor CTC's performance and recommend service enhancements to customers. The Account Care System lets customer care specialists review installed services, initiate and keep track of repair and service work, and review past billing. Information is fed to a customer history file, while orders and service requests are fed to the Provisioning System. The Provisioning System is electronically linked to suppliers' systems and, in conjunction with the Account Care System, tracks orders and notes any problems. When an order is filled, information is fed to the Billing System.

The Billing System is actually an innovative cost management tool that gives CTC a big edge over its competition. Bills are available on diskette and CD-ROM as well as paper, and can be sorted by length of call, calls to a certain number or area code, calls from a certain extension, and more. Customers have on-line access to their CTC billing and account information. Just as important, this single bill includes all of a customer's telecommunications charges. CTC's immediate plans include enhancing its services and providing its customers with the capability to order, report problems, review services, and pay bills on-line.

### Looking Forward to the Future

CTC has aggressive plans for the approach of the new millennium. Steve Milton, CTC's president and COO, says the company intends to add 20 additional branches over a three-year period. In addition to opening three offices in New York State, CTC has opened an office in Maryland, and plans to expand into New Jersey, Virginia, and Washington, D.C. By mid-1999,

CTC will have 240 account executives operating from 27 branches—a 30 percent increase in less than one year.

Milton is equally excited by the second front of CTC's growth: the building of an integrated, data-centric, carrier-grade network. "This network will provide our customers with dedicated T-1 or other broadband access to the network, and will bundle an integrated package of data and voice services," says Milton. "Our phase one network deployment includes 12 hubs within New York, New Jersey, and New England, and will be operational in the summer of 1999." With its intelligent approach to expansion and enlightened approach to customer service, CTC looks forward to continuing success for many years to come.

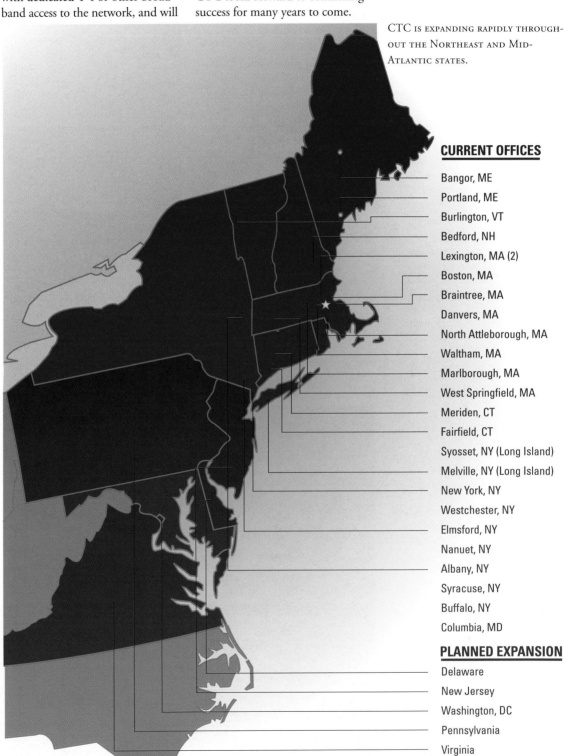

CTC IS EXPANDING RAPIDLY THROUGHOUT THE NORTHEAST AND MID-ATLANTIC STATES.

## CURRENT OFFICES

Bangor, ME
Portland, ME
Burlington, VT
Bedford, NH
Lexington, MA (2)
Boston, MA
Braintree, MA
Danvers, MA
North Attleborough, MA
Waltham, MA
Marlborough, MA
West Springfield, MA
Meriden, CT
Fairfield, CT
Syosset, NY (Long Island)
Melville, NY (Long Island)
New York, NY
Westchester, NY
Elmsford, NY
Nanuet, NY
Albany, NY
Syracuse, NY
Buffalo, NY
Columbia, MD

## PLANNED EXPANSION

Delaware
New Jersey
Washington, DC
Pennsylvania
Virginia

# Pro Media, Inc.

PRO MEDIA, INC., ONE OF THE NATION'S LARGEST INDEPENDENT media planning and buying firms, is headquartered in Natick. Founded in 1980 by its president and CEO Nancy Ryan, Pro Media has grown to $200 million in media billings, currently employing more than 50 media specialists. Under Ryan's guidance, Pro Media lives up to its mission statement of "providing

advertisers with the best strategic media planning and buying in today's ever changing media universe."

Pro Media's wide range of services, which take a marketing-driven approach, is designed to help clients maximize every advertising dollar they spend. These services include strategic planning and media buying, market analysis, market research, competitive landscape studies, promotions, event and sports marketing, post-buy analysis, and material trafficking.

"Strategic thinking, state-of-the-art technology and research applications, and the top media professionals in the business, give Pro Media its competitive edge," says Ryan. "Pro Media strives to deliver the most exciting and efficient media buys, and we accomplish this every day with our dedicated and very talented staff. Rosemary Petta, executive vice president of media services, is committed to our

business philosophy and has been responsible for Pro Media's media services for more than 18 years."

Providing excellent customer service is paramount in Pro Media's business model and is a key contributor in its success. Pro Media's executive vice president of account

service, Susan Ryan, states, "Advertisers spend the vast majority of their budgets on media placement. The Account Service department at Pro Media is charged with managing all communication and direction relative to an advertiser's needs. We do this by immersing ourselves in each client's business." This business strategy also sets Pro Media apart from its competitors.

For its clients, Pro Media develops integrated media plans that distinguish their advertising message in a very crowded marketplace. Working in tandem with a client's in-house marketing and advertising department, Pro Media establishes media objectives and goals that provide the platform for successful advertising campaigns. Pro Media always looks to achieve the desired results, both short- and long-term.

Core competencies in broadcast and cable television media buying include national, syndication, and

ot. Radio expertise encompasses twork, syndicated, wired, and wired networks as well as spot. significant percentage of Pro edia's billing is derived from its int advertisers. Active in virtually percent of the United States at y given time, Pro Media places vertising in national, regional, d local magazines and newspa-rs. In addition, the company has st experience with inserts, free-nding inserts (FSIs), couponing, d all out-of-home media such as tdoor and transit.

Pro Media has recently estab-hed a separate division called Minteractive. This media com-ny addresses the interactive ying and planning needs of its ents and has in a short time far ceeded its first year's goals.

Nancy Ryan notes that Pro edia has grown steadily as its cli-ts have grown. The company's ent roster includes prestigious tional and regional advertisers, any of which have a long-term lationship with Pro Media. These ents include Staples The Office perstore, WCVB-TV, MVP orts, and HP Hood. In addition consumer clients, the company s developed a substantial political vision in which advertising for

political candidates and ballot ref-erenda is planned and placed.

Finally, financial accountability has been the mainstay of Pro Media's managed growth. Les Greenberg, executive vice president and CFO, states, "We spend a great deal of client funds each year, and finan-cial trust is vital to the overall solid business relationship we enjoy with each of our clients. We spend a significant amount of time and energy ensuring that our clients receive the best media placement efforts to reach their target audience with their advertising message— and just as much effort in account-ing for their dollars."

Pro Media's involvement in com-munity and civic activities has also grown over the years, and is some-thing that is strongly encouraged on a companywide basis. "From a company standpoint, we believe that we have an obligation to give something back and, as individuals, we all believe that one person's ef-forts can make a difference," explains Marie Lowre, vice president of administration. "Whether it is vol-unteering during the holidays to provide Thanksgiving meals or serv-ing on the boards of various chari-ties, the company response is always positive and it speaks volumes about how special our people are."

# Stratus Computer, Inc.

CHARGE A MEAL OR A HOTEL BILL, DO BANKING OVER THE INTERNE purchase a lottery ticket—whether people are in Boston or L Vegas, Tokyo, or London, chances are a fault-tolerant Strat computer is handling their transactions. ❧ Stratus Computer, Inc founded in 1980, is the premier supplier of computer systems ar services where continuous availability is a critical need. The

systems and services enable Stratus customers to run the most critical parts of their business while maintaining the highest level of system and application availability. In turn, this helps Stratus customers provide better service to their own customers.

For years, Stratus has directed its focus on the critical end of business to the advantage of companies located around the world. More than 950 Stratus employees—based in company headquarters in the Greater Boston area and at other sites worldwide—have the training and experience to develop solutions for industries as diverse as financial services, health care, travel/trans-

portation, and manufacturing, among others.

## Setting the Standards

Stock markets and other global companies have greatly benefited from the continuously available services Stratus provides for their mission-critical operations. The company's focus on these crucial segments of the business world has set a new standard in business computing.

Stratus offers a high-performance, flexible suite of products that has brought a new standard of system availability to worldwide businesses. Stratus computers are designed to

enable businesses to bring operations on-line quickly; protect thei investments; run business-critical operations 24 hours a day, 365 days a year; and expand or enhan these services as market or busine: conditions demand.

The company also offers a wide selection of operating systen and industry-standard communic tions and networking capabilities. Through its extensive list of third party partners, Stratus provides an array of industry-specific appli cation software, development plat forms, and messaging middlewar

But even the most robust solu tions need safeguarding. To ensu

IT MIGHT BE A SINGLE, MULTIMILLION-DOLLAR ELECTRONIC FUNDS TRANSFER, OR A FLOOD OF TRADING ACTIVITY AT THE CLOSE OF THE BUSINESS DAY. BANKS, BROKERAGE HOUSES, AND OTHER FINAN-CIAL SERVICES COMPANIES DEPEND ON STRATUS TO KEEP THE MONEY MOVING SECURELY.

Bosto

...at customers' operations stay up and running at all times, Stratus created a worldwide network of Customer Assistance Centers. The centers are run by service professionals who can resolve system and application software problems, and dispatch replacement parts, which customers can easily insert into their systems without interrupting operations.

Stratus also offers remote on-line service in which the client's computer can perform self-diagnostics to detect problems and then "phone home" to the Customer Assistance Center. Stratus was the first company to offer this type of remote service. It is not uncommon for a customer who receives a replacement part to call the Customer Assistance Center and inquire why

the part has been sent to his or her firm. Stratus is able to detect an error or potential failure before the customer realizes there is a problem and before any interruption occurs.

Stratus has both indirect and direct sales operations in locations worldwide. The firm also has an extensive list of value-added resellers, distributors, and systems integrators.

CLOCKWISE FROM TOP LEFT: STRATUS CONTINUOUS PROCESSING IS BUILT AROUND THE CONCEPT THAT ALL ASPECTS OF THE SYSTEM DESIGN MUST BE ADDRESSED TO CREATE A SYSTEM THAT IS CONTINUOUSLY AVAILABLE. STRATUS PROVIDES DUPLEX HARDWARE, OPERATING SYSTEM KERNEL HARDENING, ON-LINE UPGRADES, AND MORE.

WHEREVER THERE IS A CRITICAL NEED, STRATUS WILL BE THERE. THE COMPANY'S SYSTEMS ENSURE THAT EMERGENCY 911 CALLS GET THROUGH 24 HOURS A DAY—WITHOUT FAIL.

BUSY TRAVELERS AROUND THE WORLD RELY ON STRATUS CONTINUOUS AVAILABILITY SYSTEMS TO STAY ON TIME AND ON LOCATION, EVERY HOUR OF EVERY DAY.

I N ANY GIVEN YEAR, MASSACHUSETTS' CONVENTION INDUSTR generates hundreds of millions of dollars for the Commonwealt Meeting and convention delegates flock to the state, spending mone on hotels, restaurants, retail stores, museums, auto rentals, and host of other activities, generating prosperity for all. ❧ Spearheadir successful efforts to attract meeting and convention business is th

GLORIA C. LARSON (TOP LEFT) IS CHAIRMAN OF THE MASSACHUSETTS CONVENTION CENTER AUTHORITY. FRANCIS X. JOYCE (BOTTOM LEFT) IS EXECUTIVE DIRECTOR OF THE MASSACHUSETTS CONVENTION CENTER AUTHORITY.

THE JOHN B. HYNES VETERANS MEMORIAL CONVENTION CENTER FEATURES 37 MEETING ROOMS, AN AUDITORIUM, AND BEAUTIFULLY APPOINTED BANQUET FACILITIES, SUCH AS THE ONE PICTURED HERE, WHICH CAN ACCOMMODATE BANQUET PARTIES OF UP TO 2,000.

Massachusetts Convention Center Authority (MCCA). The MCCA was formed in 1982, with a mission to bolster Massachusetts' economic vitality by attracting meeting and convention business to the state. Today, the MCCA owns and operates the John B. Hynes Veterans Memorial Convention Center (the Hynes), Boston's landmark meeting and convention facility, and the Springfield Civic Center (the Civic Center), located in Massachusetts' third-largest city. Additionally, the MCCA is overseeing development of the Boston Convention & Exhibition Center (BCEC). Together, these properties will form the nucleus of Massachusetts' convention business in the new millennium.

The MCCA operates under the guidance of Francis X. Joyce, who has served as executive director since the organization's inception. During his tenure, the state's meeting and convention business has thrived, fueling substantial job creation and, for Greater Boston hotels, record room occupancy and room rates. Joyce reports to a 13-member board of gubernatorial and mayoral appointees chaired by Gloria Larson, who was appointed at a critical transitional period, as the MCCA began overseeing development of the BCEC. Upon completion, the BCEC will be New England's largest meeting and convention facility and a boon to the economy.

## The Hynes—A Thriving Back Bay Landmark

Touring Boston's tony Back Bay, it's difficult to miss the Hynes. With its classic facade—the Hynes has been recognized for architectural excellence—the facility stands out in a neighborhood populated by boutiques, restaurants, shopping galleries, and hotels. One of the most striking aspects of the

neighborhood is that virtually every convenience is within walking distance, supporting Boston's famous moniker—America's Walking City.

The predecessor to the Hynes, the War Memorial Auditorium, opened in 1965. Featuring 150,000 square feet of exhibit space and a 5,826-seat auditorium, the facility was considered leading edge for its time. By the 1980s, however, Boston was ripe for a facility capable of accommodating larger-scale meetings and conventions—a rapidly growing and lucrative business. Recognizing this, state officials set about the task of renovating the auditorium and positioning it to compete for domestic and international meeting and convention business. The result? The Hynes.

Since reopening in 1988 under the guidance of the MCCA, the Hynes has enjoyed great success and a reputation as one of the world's leading convention facilities. Its popularity is at least partly due to its superior amenities and location. Boasting 193,000 square feet of exhibition space, 37 dedicated meeting rooms, an auditorium, and a ballroom, the Hynes is ideal for delegations of up to nearly 25,000. Reflecting current business needs, the Hynes features state-of-the-art technology supported by on-site

technicians, enabling global connectivity while meeting in Boston

Another form of connectivity—to the city's hotels, shops, and restaurants—is equally vital. The Hynes delivers on all counts. As anchor of the Boston Convention Complex (BCC)—a unique partnership—the Hynes is interconnected by a series of glass-enclosed walkways with the Sheraton Bosto Hotel, the Boston Marriott Hotel Copley Place, and the Westin Cople Place; more than 200 shops; a cinema complex; and restaurants in two upscale shopping arcades. A virtual city within a city, the BCC lets delegates attend a meeting, dine, and repose in one of 3,000 luxury hotel rooms without ever stepping outside.

## The Boston Convention & Exhibition Center— A Link to the Future

Across town, the historic Seaport District is experienc ing a renaissance. In its heyday, the district was a hub for Boston's maritime industries. In the next few years, the Seaport will bustle anew with offices, restaurants, and the BCEC.

The BCEC, targeted for comple tion in 2003, will anchor the revitalized Seaport District. The $700

Airport

Downtown

New BCEC site

TOP LEFT: THE JOHN B. HYNES VETERANS MEMORIAL CONVENTION CENTER (LOCATED IN BACKGROUND OF THIS PHOTO) IS ONE OF THE WORLD'S PREMIER MEETING AND CONVENTION FACILITIES. THE CENTER IS LOCATED IN BOSTON'S BACK BAY, NESTLED AMONG BROWNSTONES, RETAIL STORES, RESTAURANTS, BOUTIQUES, HOTELS, AND SHOPPING ARCADES.

BOTTOM LEFT: THIS AERIAL VIEW SHOWS THE FUTURE SITE OF THE BOSTON CONVENTION & EXHIBITION CENTER. UPON COMPLETION, THE FACILITY WILL FEATURE 600,000 SQUARE FEET OF CONTIGUOUS EXHIBITION SPACE ON ONE LEVEL, MEETING ROOMS, BANQUET FACILITIES, AND MORE, MAKING IT THE CENTERPIECE OF THE MASSACHUSETTS CONVENTION CENTER AUTHORITY'S PORTFOLIO OF MEETING AND CONVENTION PROPERTIES.

Springfield officials launched a five-year, $100 million revitalization effort aimed at improving the city's 17 neighborhoods, downtown, and riverfront. At the center of the newly refurbished Springfield is the Civic Center, itself the subject of a renovation currently in the planning stages under the guidance of the MCCA.

The Civic Center's pre-renovation specifications include 65,000 total square feet of space; a 10,000-seat arena with an adjacent 40,000-square-foot exhibit hall; a 7,000-square-foot banquet hall; and five meeting rooms. The facility is located near three downtown hotels with more than 800 rooms and within 18 miles of Bradley International Airport in Windsor Locks, Connecticut.

After renovation, the Civic Center will have a state-of-the-art arena and 80,000 square feet of exhibition space and meeting rooms. With this latest boost, Springfield is poised to attract a larger share of the meeting and convention market.

SPRINGFIELD, THE THIRD-LARGEST CITY IN THE COMMONWEALTH, IS SITUATED IN THE PIONEER VALLEY OF WESTERN MASSACHUSETTS. AT THE CENTER OF THE CITY IS THE SPRINGFIELD CIVIC CENTER, WHICH WILL FEATURE A 10,000-SEAT ARENA AND 80,000 SQUARE FEET OF EXHIBIT AND BANQUET SPACE, JUST A SHORT JAUNT FROM 800 DOWNTOWN HOTEL ROOMS.

million facility, featuring 600,000 square feet of contiguous exhibition space on one level, provides Boston with enormous potential to attract larger association and trade show events. More important, it gives organizers of large meetings another reason to locate in a city consistently identified as one of the most desirable destinations in the world, and assures that the MCCA will continue to play an important role in the economic development of Massachusetts into the next millennium.

A five-minute drive from Logan Airport, the BCEC will be convenient to Boston's rapid transit lines—the subway system is being

extended to reach the new center—and the Massachusetts Turnpike. And visitors to the area will have a clear view and easy access on foot to Faneuil Hall and other downtown attractions, as a result of the relocation of the Central Artery underground.

## The Springfield Civic Center— A Convention Alternative in Western Massachusetts

In the Pioneer Valley of western Massachusetts, along the Connecticut border, is Springfield, home of the Civic Center. Located along the Connecticut River, Springfield is just a 90-minute drive on Interstate 90 from Boston. In 1993,

# Saville Systems PLC

A LL THE RULES HAVE CHANGED IN THE NEWLY DEREGULATED world of telecommunications and energy. Where previously there were highly profitable, if regulated, national telecommunications and energy authorities, now there are wide-open, highly competitive environments with multiple competitors slugging it out for a piece of the action in the global market. The keys to

success in this Darwinian fray are technical prowess and meticulous customer service. Sophisticated technology is an absolute must, because customers will accept nothing less. With so many vendors offering cutting-edge technology, this is a tough area in which to establish a competitive advantage. However, when it comes to customer service, there are huge competitive advantages to be gained by resourceful companies willing to develop innovative, customer-friendly strategies.

Saville is such a company. Founded in 1982, the firm employs more than 1,400 professionals, including 750 telecommunications applications experts with hundreds of years of collective experience in the telecommunications billing industry.

Saville—which is based in the Boston suburb of Burlington and has offices throughout the Americas, Europe, and Asia—made its initial public offering in November 1995, and since that time has racked up

a string of 13 consecutive record-breaking quarters. The company's 1997 revenues of $107 million and net income of $23.9 million were up 99 percent and 107 percent, respectively, from 1996. The firm's workhorse family of products is its modular Saville CBP (convergent billing platform), which integrates information on the multiple services offered by telephone and energy companies and creates a convergent bill.

According to Saville Chairman and CEO Jack Boyle, the company has realized its financial success by carefully blending savvy business acumen with topflight technology and excellent customer service. "Having been around as long as we have, Saville knows that the only way to prosper in the customer care and billing industry is by always looking ahead, while keeping an eye on the present," Boyle notes. "By maintaining this kind of balance, we are always prepared for the changing needs of our customers."

As the first vendor to offer convergent customer care and billing software systems for telecommunications service providers, Saville garnered a large slice of market share that it has never relinquished, due to its cutting-edge technology and its intensive focus on the customer. That focus is exemplified by the large amount of time Saville executives spend on the road meeting with customers personally.

## Convergent Customer Care and Billing

S aville's integrated customer care and billing solutions are mission-critical applications that enable telecommunications and energy providers such as AT&T, Sprint, Time Warner, Global One, Exelon Energy, and their counter-

BASED IN THE BOSTON SUBURB OF BURLINGTON, SAVILLE HAS OFFICES THROUGHOUT THE AMERICAS, EUROPE, AND ASIA. THE COMPANY HAS REALIZED ITS FINANCIAL SUCCESS BY CAREFULLY BLENDING SAVVY BUSINESS ACUMEN WITH TOP-FLIGHT TECHNOLOGY AND EXCELLENT CUSTOMER SERVICE.

rts around the world not only to tegrate bills for multiple services, it also to respond quickly to aggressive competitors by getting new oducts and services to market rapidly as possible. For example, Saville customer may want to eate a bundle of services that includes Internet long distance. Or, e customer may want to offer scounted long-distance service r customers who spend a certain nount of money each month.

Most telecommunications and ergy service providers have inefficient billing systems that can't be sily modified or enhanced because ey are based on homegrown des and dated hardware. These utdated billing systems significntly delay their reaction time hen competitors announce new icing programs. Convergent cusmer care and billing form the rnerstone of Saville's success, d create a strategic bulwark for ville's customers. Because Saville ables its customers to bill multiple rvices on a single invoice, those stomers have gained an advantage at allows them to bring new serces to market without changing eir billing systems.

"Working with Saville is truly a win-win situation," says Robert Hyer, billing process manager at AT&T. "The people are highly customer focused, flexible, and very responsive. Their deep commitment and knowledge of both the telecommunications and technology aspects of our business make it easy to work with them to develop a comprehensive system that meets all our needs."

According to market researcher Gartner Group, the market for billing and customer care systems is expected to reach $9 billion by 2002. Deregulating markets in telecommunications and energy around the world represent lucrative opportunities for Saville. The energy market is especially enticing because deregulated energy utilities will be able to offer local and long-distance telecommunications services in direct competition with existing carriers who have long enjoyed monopolistic control. Saville is aggressively pursuing this emerging market.

## "It's Your Business"

In addition to looking outward at its customers, Saville also focuses inwardly on its own em-

ployees through its Saville College of Billing Knowledge. This intense, college-level, six- to eight-week course details the issues surrounding telecommunications and energy industry billing. Taught by instructors with a minimum of 10 years of industry experience, this course is also taken by experienced professionals, who use it to refresh their knowledge.

Saville is also dedicated to maintaining ongoing communications with its employees after they graduate from the Saville College of Billing Knowledge. This dedication spawned the idea for It's Your Business, an internal electronic newsletter/bulletin board, anchored by a monthly commentary from Boyle, that is only available to Saville employees.

"We realize how important it is to keep in touch with our employees and have them know what's going on with the senior management team," says Boyle. "We created It's Your Business for our employees because Saville *is* their business, and we want them to feel a part of it every day. The more informed they are, the more able they are to maximize their performance."

INCE ITS FOUNDING IN 1983—LONG BEFORE THE INTERNET became a driving force in our lives—Banyan Systems Incorporated has been a pioneer and leader in computer networks. Banyan's products and services are used by nearly half of the Fortune 1,000. Its largest customers include the federal government and leading companies in the financial services, transportation, public utility, and manufacturing industries. Headquartered in Westboro, "Banyan was instrumental in establishing the important role that distributed networks play in business and government today," says Bill Ferry, who took over as Banyan's chairman and chief executive officer in 1997. "The company is now leading the way in utilizing directory technology and services to enable enterprise networks to use the Internet to cost effectively expand their reach to customers, suppliers, distribution partners, and mobile employees today and into the future," says Ferry.

The proliferation of the Internet has changed the way people communicate and has expanded the traditional corporate network into a worldwide communications vehicle. Banyan has kept pace with the popularity of the Internet by expanding its product and service solutions. A major part of the company's transition to the Internet era has been delivering new standards-based technology, products, and services. Banyan's solutions connect and integrate diverse computing resources into a global network. Increasingly, these resources are the basis for conducting business with customers, suppliers, dealers, and mobile employees over the Internet. "Banyan is uniquely positioned to provide proven, directory-based network security, administration, and management for business applications being deployed on the Web," says Ferry.

### Innovative Products and Services

Today, Banyan's three main focuses are networking software, network services, and Switchboard, its majority-owned Internet subsidiary and leading directory service on the Web (www.switchboard.com). The company's enterprise directory software product is StreetTalk® for Windows NT®, a directory service for the Microsoft Windows NT networking environment. The StreetTalk directory service enables people to locate and share information easily across computer networks. Today, there are more than 8 million StreetTalk users worldwide. Banyan also develops and sells software for World Wide Web servers and intranets, an E-mail product called BeyondMail®, and the VINES® network operating system, which integrates powerful messaging and network management capabilities with StreetTalk.

Banyan's consulting and support services business includes directory-enabled application design and implementation, new technology integration, transition services, and operations support. Included in transition services are offerings to help companies prepare their computer networking systems to properly handle the year 2000.

Switchboard is the Internet's leading on-line directory service with more than 120 million residential and business listings. Switchboard's president, Dean Polnerow, says, "When we launched Switchboard in 1996, our objective was to advance Internet directory technology by an order of magnitude." In 1997, Switchboard's Web site was named the fastest-growing Internet directory service by Media Metrix, and is one of the top 20 most-visited sites on the World Wide Web, receiving nearly 100 million yellow and white page inquiries per month.

As a free service to Internet users, Switchboard has an advertising-based revenue model. The Web site features display advertisements that are integrated with its business listings and that are categorized to match a user's search criteria. Switchboard conducts advertising business with many of the top 100 Web advertisers, including Microsoft, 800-Flowers, Barnes & Noble, and CDnow. SideClick® is Switchboard's innovative Web-searching service. Switchboard has also been awarded two patents for privacy technology. The site's "knock-knock" feature protects Internet users from "spam" mail—unsolicited messages equivalent to junk mail.

In addition to providing a service, Polnerow says, "I believe that we've brought thousands of people together that had no other way to find each other. I get mail messages all the time from people who have found lost relatives, college friends, or military buddies they haven't spoken to in 25 years."

Publicly held and traded on the Nasdaq stock exchange, Banyan's 1997 revenues exceeded $73 million. Employing more than 400 people worldwide, the company has nearly 40 sales and support offices in major cities in the United States, Canada, the United Kingdom, France, Germany, the Netherlands, Australia, Malaysia, and Japan. The Westboro headquarters houses research and development, manufacturing and distribution, and operations for Switchboard.

Banyan is a company on the move with plans to expand its network product initiatives, network services, and Switchboard. To help fund this future growth, in 1998, the company completed a $10 million equity investment from HarbourVest Partners, LLC, one of the largest private equity investment firms in the world.

Ferry says, "By focusing our core competencies on these three rapidly growing markets, Banyan will steadily grow its business by becoming a leading provider of directory-based business solutions."

directory

intuitive

.com

integration

*networking*

@

SECURITY

*password*

browser

*migration*

WWW//

**O**VERLOOKING HISTORIC, ELEGANT EUROPEAN BROWNSTONES, The Westin Copley Place Boston provides splendid views of Copley Square, the Charles River, the city's financial district, and Boston Harbor. The 800-room, 36-floor, upscale hotel offers a grandeur of both size and decor—two magnificent waterfalls welcome guests into the lobby—while maintaining the charm

THE 800-ROOM, 36-FLOOR WESTIN COPLEY PLACE BOSTON OFFERS A GRANDEUR OF BOTH SIZE AND DECOR— TWO MAGNIFICENT WATERFALLS WELCOME GUESTS INTO THE LOBBY—WHILE MAINTAINING THE CHARM AND PERSONALITY OF AN INTIMATE GETAWAY FOR LEISURE AND BUSINESS TRAVELERS (TOP).

FROM THE CONTEMPORARY SOUNDS OF JAZZ TO THE ELEGANT, SPACIOUS GUEST ROOMS TO THE SUMPTUOUS MEALS TO THE UNPARALLELED CUSTOMER SERVICE, THE WESTIN COPLEY PLACE BOSTON HAS MUCH TO OFFER (BOTTOM).

and personality of an intimate getaway for leisure and business travelers. And the hotel's fashionable address puts guests in the heart of cosmopolitan Boston.

The Westin Copley Place Boston is part of the Westin Hotels & Resorts brand, which in 1997 was named the number one upscale hotel chain for the business traveler by *Frequent Flyer* magazine/J.D. Power and Associates. And for four consecutive years, Westin Hotels & Resorts has been recognized as the number one upscale hotel chain by readers of *Business Travel News.* Founded as Western Hotels on August 27, 1930, the company has grown from having 17 hotels in the Pacific Northwest to becoming a global management, marketing, franchise, technical, and reservations services business with more than 85 properties in 23 countries. In 1998, Westin was acquired by Starwood Hotels & Resorts.

## Paving the Way for Copley Square

The Westin Copley Place Boston, which opened its doors in 1983, paved the way for the development of the Copley Square area, and serves as the anchor to the trendy South End neighbor-

hood. Travelers staying at the contemporary hotel—a AAA four-diamond award winner—are within walking distance of many of Boston's popular and historic sites, such as Newbury Street (Boston's answer to Rodeo Drive), the Boston Common and Public Gardens, Beacon Hill, and Faneuil Hall Marketplace. Skybridges connect the hotel to world-class shopping at Copley Place and the Prudential Center, as well as to the Hynes Convention Center. The hotel is four miles from Logan International Airport, and is located across the street from both the Back Bay and Copley Square subway stations.

All of the hotel's 800 rooms, which include 44 suites, feature a private voice-mail system, a dual-line speakerphone with dataport, on-command video, remote-controlled color television with free cable access, refreshment centers, and other amenities such as coffeemakers, ironing board and iron, hair dryers, and bathrobes. The fifth-floor fitness center features an indoor swimming and lap pool, whirlpool, sauna, men's and women's locker rooms, Stairmasters, Trotter treadmills, stationary bikes, Cybex weight equipment, state-of-the-art steppers, and free weights.

For the business traveler, The Westin Copley Place Boston features 23 meeting rooms totaling 47,000 square feet, five specialty/hospitality suites, and 28 guest offices. In addition, the entire hotel is wired with T1 and T3 lines for fast Internet access. The Staffordshire Room, overlooking Trinity Church in Copley Square, accommodates dinner parties of 200. And the America Ballroom, one of the city's largest function rooms, can hold events of up to 2,000 people. Industry recognition for The Westin Copley Place's meetings and busi-

WARREN JAGGER PHOTOGRAPHY, INC.

WARREN JAGGER PHOTOGRAPHY, INC.

ss facilities include 13 consecutive nnacle Awards for Successful eetings, the Planners Choice ward from *Meeting News* in 1997, d *Corporate & Incentive Travel*'s ward of Excellence in 1997. The estin's Executive Club Level fers private check-in, a personal ncierge, and a lounge with comimentary continental breakfast d evening hospitality, as well as E-mail and Internet workstation.

### ward-Winning Services

he hotel prides itself on its customer service—which starts th greeting each guest by name— d a staff dedicated to providing a gh-quality experience. In 1997, *here Magazine* named one of the ormen at The Westin Copley ace Boston Guest Ambassador the Year. In 1998, the American otel and Motel Association named

one of the hotel's associates Lodging Employee of the Year, and the hotel's banquet captain received the Spirited Service Award from the Greater Boston Convention and Visitors Bureau.

Fine dining is another source of pride for The Westin Copley Place Boston. The hotel's chefs hail from all corners of the globe, including Switzerland and Austria, and bring the flavors of the world to Boston. The hotel's restaurants include the Palm, New York's legendary steakhouse, and Turner Fisheries of Boston, both of which have received Best of Boston awards from *Boston Magazine*. In addition, Turner Fisheries has won the New England Chowderfest so often, it's been elected to the Chowderfest Hall of Fame.

Guest services at The Westin Copley Place Boston include

24-hour room service, a men's barbershop, full-service business center, laundry and valet services, multilingual concierge and hotel staff, 24-hour valet and indoor garage parking, automobile rental services on premise, and foreign currency exchange.

### Helping the Community

The Westin Copley Place Boston, in addition to contributing to the city's economy and surrounding businesses, has also been an active supporter of many civic and cultural organizations. The hotel supports Community Servings, which provides meals to people living with AIDS, and was recently honored for its involvement with Second Helpings, a program that donates food to homeless shelters in the city. In addition, hotel employees have served Thanksgiving dinner each year for residents of the Boston Living Center.

In conjunction with the live jazz that is featured in the lounge at Turner Fisheries, and in the spirit of promoting the arts, The Westin Copley Place Boston has provided a number of grants to students at Boston's Berklee College of Music. The hotel is also a corporate supporter of the Boston Ballet and the Boston Symphony.

From the contemporary sounds of jazz to the elegant, spacious guest rooms to the sumptuous meals to the unparalleled customer service, The Westin Copley Place Boston has much to offer.

THE WESTIN COPLEY PLACE BOSTON IS PART OF THE WESTIN HOTELS & RESORTS BRAND, WHICH IN 1997 WAS NAMED THE NUMBER ONE UPSCALE HOTEL CHAIN FOR THE BUSINESS TRAVELER BY *Frequent Flyer* MAGAZINE/ J.D. POWER AND ASSOCIATES.

FOR THE BUSINESS TRAVELER, THE WESTIN COPLEY PLACE BOSTON FEATURES 23 MEETING ROOMS TOTALING 47,000 SQUARE FEET, FIVE SPECIALTY/ HOSPITALITY SUITES, AND 28 GUEST OFFICES.

ESTLED IN THE HEART OF BOSTON'S HISTORIC BACK BAY— an area where history, business, art, culture, and upscale shopping converge—is the Boston Marriott Copley Place. With its elegant, five-story atrium lobby lit by a grand chandelier; first-class accommodations for both the corporate and the individual traveler; sharp attention to service; and New

England's largest ballroom, the Boston Marriott Copley Place lives up to its billing as "a world-class hotel for a world-class city."

The anchor hotel in Boston's 9.5-acre Copley Place development, the Boston Marriott Copley Place opened its doors in May 1984, and today, it serves 7,000 guests per week. The hotel boasts 1,147 guest rooms—250 of which have been designed specifically for business travelers—and 47 suites. The rooms are continuously upgraded and renovated for the latest in guest comfort and technology.

### State-of-the-Art Amenities

The Boston Marriott's amenities include a full-service health club with state-of-the-art exercise equipment, indoor pool, sauna, whirlpool, and massage therapy. In addition, there are two concierge levels for guest courtesies.

Within the hotel are six restaurants: Gourmeli's, which serves American favorites; Champions, a sports bar with live entertainment and casual fare; Bello Mondo, which serves Northern Italian cuisine; the Sushi Bar; the Gourmet Bean coffee shop; and the Terrace Lounge, which features cocktails, light fare, and quiet entertainment.

For visitors to Boston, the hotel is conveniently located just four miles from Logan Airport, and is connected by climate-controlled, covered walkways to more than 200 fine shops, restaurants, and movie theaters at the nearby Copley Place and Prudential shopping centers.

### Ideal for Business Meetings

For the business traveler and corporate groups and functions, Boston Marriott Copley Place offers extensive facilities and leading technology. A member of

WITH ITS ELEGANT, FIVE-STORY ATRIUM LOBBY LIT BY A GRAND CHANDELIER; FIRST-CLASS ACCOMMODATIONS FOR BOTH THE CORPORATE AND THE INDIVIDUAL TRAVELER; SHARP ATTENTION TO SERVICE; AND NEW ENGLAND'S LARGEST BALLROOM, THE BOSTON MARRIOTT COPLEY PLACE LIVES UP TO ITS BILLING AS "A WORLD-CLASS HOTEL FOR A WORLD-CLASS CITY."

the Marriott Meetings Network, the hotel features more than 60,000 square feet of meeting and exhibit space on three consecutive levels. In addition, the hotel's 22,500-square-foot exhibit hall accommodates up to 145 booths measuring eight feet by 10 feet. High-speed Internet access via T-3 lines is permanently wired into all 34 meeting rooms and the exhibit hall. The hotel is connected by an enclosed walkway to the Prudential Center complex and the Hynes Convention Center.

Business groups can also utilize the on-site Business Center and the hotel's technical support staff. Boston Marriott Copley Place, in addition to catering, offers corporate groups theme party options including New England clambakes.

For both its leisure and its business guests, Boston Marriott Copley Place is "dedicated to providing the Marriott brand of hospitality," says General Manager Bill Munck. "Our mission is to make sure every guest leaves our hotel satisfied."

OSTON'S FORT POINT CHANNEL AREA—WHICH IS IN THE MIDST OF being transformed from a district of old textile buildings into a new and vibrant economic hub—is an ideal location for fast-growing Payton Construction Corporation. The full-service construction firm, established in 1986 by William B. Payton, president, relocated to its new, 20,000-square-foot headquarters

in the spring of 1998, having outgrown its two previous Boston locations.

Payton Construction first opened for business with a staff of only Bill Payton and a secretary. Today, it is a $110 million company with 70 employees, including project managers, estimators, accountants, marketing professionals, and field superintendents. The company is on the march, expanding from its traditional downtown Boston market to the surrounding suburbs, New England, and beyond. In late 1997, Payton Construction opened an office in Portland, Maine, and the firm is also working in Philadelphia.

### Forging a Reputation

Payton Construction offers general contracting services, construction management services, reconstruction consulting, and design/build services to a wide range of clients. These include health care facilities and laboratories, colleges and universities, religious facilities, major corporations, financial institutions, retailers, building owners and managers, and tenants. The company has many repeat clients, which Bill Payton attributes to the firm's focus on quality and service.

In Payton Construction's early days, the company established a reputation for its commercial office build-outs, taking the lead on many of the larger renovations in downtown Boston. Since then, the company has completed millions of square feet of tenant renovations, establishing long-standing relationships with well-known Boston institutions such as Fidelity, the Boston Stock Exchange, Harvard University, Massachusetts General Hospital, and the property managers, Rose Associates.

Payton's recent expansion into the new construction market in-

cludes projects such as the Robert McBride House in Boston, a 19,700-square-foot, six-story independent living facility for people with AIDS; a 65,000-square-foot Super Stop & Shop, straddling the borders of Salem and Peabody; and Temple Shir Tikva's 28,000-square-foot, two-story education facility in Wayland.

Payton Construction has received numerous honors and awards over the years. Most recently, Payton's restoration of the Exeter Street Theatre building—a century-old Boston landmark devastated by fire in 1995—earned the firm the 1997 Associated General Contractors' Build Massachusetts Honor Award. On the scene while the flames were still smoldering, the Payton team assessed the damage and secured the building. The $9 million restoration, completed over the next year, employed a unique combination of state-of-the-art computer technology and century-old jacking techniques to reinforce the building's structure. Payton also located rare Munson slate to replace the roof tiles lost to fire; conducted extensive, emergency repairs to original masonry; and carefully preserved the landmark copper-clad cupola in order to build and install an accurate copy.

### Building the Community

Payton Construction has also established itself as a generous contributor to Boston's community through pro bono projects. The firm funded and facilitated the build-out of a much-needed larger office for Make-A-Wish Foundation of Greater Boston on Devonshire Street. The company also has donated the services of its personnel to the Neighborhood House Charter School in Dorchester for restoration of the unused convent at St. Mark's Church.

Bill Payton, a Massachusetts native, is an active participant in the community and industry, serving on the board of directors for Make-A-Wish Foundation, Associated General Contractors, and Massachusetts Building Congress.

### Into the Future

New construction and geographic expansion will continue to be growth areas for the company in the coming years. Says Payton, "I am most proud of the company's growth, the people who work here, and the respect we've received from both employees and clients."

PAYTON CONSTRUCTION'S PROJECTS INCLUDE (CLOCKWISE FROM TOP) PAYTON CONSTRUCTION CORPORATION HEADQUARTERS IN BOSTON, THE AWARD-WINNING EXETER STREET THEATRE BUILDING RESTORATION IN BOSTON, AND THE TENANT RENOVATION FOR LOIS PAUL & PARTNERS IN BURLINGTON, MASSACHUSETTS.

HERE'S SOMETHING A LITTLE BIT DIFFERENT ABOUT THE ADVERTISing agency of Holland Mark Martin Edmund. For starters, the firm's name consists of the middle—not last—names of its partners. The firm's Web site literally screams when visitors reach the home page, and the partners worry about their souls. Through the wisdom of such unconventional methodology, the firm remains committed to real and measurable results that deliver business for its clients.

What's going on here? Bill Davis, founder and CEO, is quick to point out that, obviously, Holland Mark Martin Edmund (HMME) is different from traditional full-service advertising agencies. "We didn't start life as an agency," he admits. "We became one accidentally. We're focused on generating a return on investment. We speak the language that CEOs speak."

## EPOC

The driving philosophy behind HMME's approach to integrated marketing communications is what the agency dubs EPOC—every point of contact. HMME's integrated marketing communications strategy is designed to build brand identities at every point of contact between the firm's clients and their customers. EPOC encompasses nearly every way the client interacts with existing and potential customers, including stationery, print and television ads, sales presentation materials, fulfillment, packaging, service, and even how the client answers the telephone. Consistency is a goal of the firm, and its partners generally feel that advertising dollars spent in isolation are ill spent.

HMME's philosophy mirrors the evolution of the agency. Davis started a direct-marketing company in 1986 called Database Marketing Corp. He was soon joined by his Connecticut College roommate, Chris Colbert, who currently serves as president of HMME. When the company's early customers, such as Polaroid, Standard & Poor's, and Honeywell, pushed Davis and Colbert to expand their services beyond direct marketing, they complied. That's when a third partner, Jack Crumbley, came on board, and the company began to expand into a full-service advertising agency.

## A Different Approach

To break with a tradition followed by nearly every other agency, the partners decided *not* to put their last names on the door, and in 1993, the firm was renamed Holland Mark Martin after the three partners' middle names. In 1996, the company moved to Boston, partly due to growth and partly for perception: Davis felt the firm needed a Boston headquarters to be taken seriously as a major player, as well as to offer more convenient access for many of its clients. The company soon added the middle name of Executive Creative Director Bob Minihan when he became a partner in 1997. In addition, HMME established a direct mail and technology division in Burlington called TPC, which is headed up by Brad Neuenhaus, president.

Today, Holland Mark Martin Edmund continues to grow, currently having 80 employees and $80 million in annual billings. Under the leadership of the partners, HMME has become the fifth-largest agency in New England. The firm provides its clients with integrated marketing communications services, including advertising, direct response, and interactive work; creative and design; media buying

TOP: HOLLAND MARK MARTIN EDMUND DESIGNED ITS OWN WEB SITE (WWW.HMME.COM) USING A COMIC BOOK METAPHOR IN WHICH CHARACTERS TAKE VISITORS ON A VIRTUAL TOUR OF THE FIRM USING SEVERAL HUMOROUS SITUATIONS.

BOTTOM: THE PARTNERS OF HOLLAND MARK MARTIN EDMUND INCLUDE (FROM LEFT) CEO BILL DAVIS, PRESIDENT CHRIS COLBERT, AND EXECUTIVE CREATIVE DIRECTOR BOB MINIHAN.

id list acquisition; new media;
ecision sciences/research and
nalytics; and full-service produc-
on management.

## aving One's Soul

There are four tenets to which
the agency remains steadfast:
o communicate with relevance
nd distinction; to be non-media-
ased, treating all disciplines equally;
o achieve real results; and to not
orfeit one's soul. The firm's part-
ers care about creating an envi-
onment for their employees that
creative, respectful, and based on
ust, and this is the same kind of
lationship the firm maintains
ith its clients.

Examples of the success of
MME's unique perspective
in be seen in the ways its clients
istinguish themselves from com-
etitors in the marketplace. For
ational client VeryFine, a juice
ompany, Davis says HMME gave
iem "a space they can own." Sell-
ig against other juice companies,
lus major soft drink brands and
ourmet waters, VeryFine is in a
rutally competitive market. What
ifferentiates the company, and
hat HMME's campaign is designed
o make consumers remember,
that VeryFine is in its fourth
eneration of family ownership:
Made by a family, not a parent
ompany." Locally, HMME was
ehind the campaign to give Boston-
ased USTrust a personality: "the
ther big bank." Says Davis, "We've
arried that through using every
oint of contact, and on a budget

probably one-50th of what their
competitors are spending."

HMME designed its own Web
site (www.hmme.com) using a comic
book metaphor in which characters
take visitors on a virtual tour of the
firm using several humorous situations. The site provides a good
example of the firm's approach to
new media and interactive technology. Explains Davis, "Most Web sites
have concept but no intent; people
go and never come back. We tried to
have a concept that gave personality
through the tour guide, to get people
to stay longer and come back."

Giving back to the community
also belongs to the soul of HMME.
Davis sits on the board of directors

of Horizons Initiative, a preschool
for homeless children; and the
International Institute of Boston,
an immigration and refugee resettle-
ment agency. Colbert is involved
in the Big Sisters organization and
is president of the Advertising Club
of Greater Boston. And employees
throughout the organization take
part in a variety of community
activities.

For all the company's accom-
plishments, Davis says he is most
proud of "how we've run the business and evolved the agency. We
spend a lot of time thinking about
people and creating a good work
environment. Everybody came here
to do smart work that gets results."

HMME HAS BECOME THE FIFTH-
LARGEST ADVERTISING AGENCY IN NEW
ENGLAND, PRODUCING WORK FOR
SUCH CLIENTS AS (CLOCKWISE FROM
TOP) BLUE CROSS AND BLUE SHIELD
OF MASSACHUSETTS, MASSACHUSETTS
OFFICE OF TRAVEL AND TOURISM, AND
*The Boston Globe*.

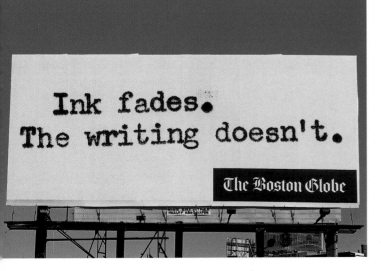

A S THE WORLDS OF WIRELESS AND WIRELINE COMMUNICATION converge, Comverse Network Systems, Inc. is in a uniqu position to provide its customers—communications networ operators and service providers across the globe—a single poir of access to the public network for a wide range of enhance services, including voice messaging and communicatior applications. With its leading-edge network products and services, Comverse Network Systems—a division of Comverse Technology, Inc.—counts among its customers the world's largest wireline and wireless operators, such as public network telephone carriers, long-distance companies, cellular providers, personal communication services (PCS) providers, cable companies, and other operators in the telecommunications industry markets.

The Comverse Network Systems division is the result of a January 1998 merger between the former Boston Technology, Inc., which was established in Wakefield in 1986, and Comverse Technology, Inc. of Woodbury, New York. Under the merger agreement, Boston Technology was combined with Comverse Technology's Network Systems Division, the company's largest operating unit. Comverse Network

Systems' headquarters remains in Wakefield. The division employs more than 3,000 people worldwide with 35 offices around the globe.

## A Truly International Company

Comverse Network Systems now offers its network customers a strong global presence and a unified messaging strategy for both wireless and wireline communications, and maintains a large portion of the industry's overall market share. Today, Comverse Network Systems delivers a full range of enhanced services solutions to more than 260 network operator customers around the world, including AT&T, Bell Atlantic, BellSouth, DDI, Deutsche Telekom, NTT, Telecom Italia, Telstra, Southwestern Bell, Sprint PCS, and TELMEX. The company has customers in 80 countries on six continents.

## Serving the Customers' Customers

Comverse Network Systems' solutions are designed to increase both customer loyalty and revenues for its network operator customers, while providing more communications options to the carriers' customers. The company's services platforms—Access NP®, TRILOGUE™ INfinity™, and ISMSC—enable communications network operators to offer a range of revenue-generating multimedia messaging and information services to business and residential users. These services include call answering, voice/fax mail, short text message service, fax on demand, audiotex, interactive voice response virtual phone/fax, and next-generation Advanced Intelligent Network based personal communications services such as prepaid services, call screening/caller introduction, and mobile attendant.

## Exporting Quality

Committed to quality, Comvers Network Systems is ISO 900 certified. In May 1998, Comverse Network Systems was presented with a Massachusetts Export Achievement Award, which recognizes companies in the state for their achievements in exporting, and helps increase awareness within the business community and the publi of the importance of international trade to the regional economy. In 1997, more than 65 percent of the company's $489 million in revenues was in exports.

In the emerging era of the convergence of telephone, Internet, television, and wireless technology, Comverse Network Systems is well positioned through its technological leadership, localized expertise, and breadth of services in a single, integrated resource.

WITH ITS LEADING-EDGE NETWORK PRODUCTS AND SERVICES, COMVERSE NETWORK SYSTEMS—A DIVISION OF COMVERSE TECHNOLOGY, INC.— COUNTS AMONG ITS CUSTOMERS THE WORLD'S LARGEST WIRELINE AND WIRELESS OPERATORS.

CID ASSOCIATES INC. IS A MULTIDISCIPLINARY ENGINEERING and architectural design firm that focuses on commercial and industrial markets. Fast-track projects, quick customer response, and a single source of both expertise and accountability are the hallmarks of this young design firm. It has successfully completed numerous projects for clients, and the job satisfaction is obvious, since nearly 80 percent are repeat customers. Clients include many of the Boston area's top property managers and development firms, architects, manufacturers, and major supermarket and food processing firms that span the geographic gamut—from Maine to Florida, Long Island to Mississippi, the eastern seaboard to Taiwan, and the Azores to Grand Cayman.

### New England Roots

The CID firm was founded on Milk Street in Boston in 1987 by three New England natives—Michael A. Cassavoy, James G. Jacobs, and John F. King Jr.—who are the firm's principals. After moving a few short months later to a larger office on Lincoln Street, the trio soon began expanding their professional staff, as well as the scope of the firm's work.

A merger in 1989 with George Manos Associates broadened CID's services to include mechanical engineering, while an Amherst-based satellite office was opened in 1994 to serve a growing client base beyond Boston. Later that year, CID moved headquarters to its present location on Summer Street. Today, the firm has 75 employees.

### Key Strengths

CID's specialized expertise includes building envelope services and historic restoration. In 1992, CID received the Massachusetts Historical Commission's Preservation Award for its building envelope services and historic restoration of the Winthrop Building—owned by Fidelity Investments—on Water Street in Boston's financial district.

More recent projects of note include New Boston Seafood, a multitenant fish-processing facility on Boston's waterfront, for which CID performed the site, architectural, mechanical, electrical, plumbing, and structural building envelope work. CID also acted as the owner's consultant for the building envelope on the recently completed Seaport Hotel in South Boston. In addition, the firm recently completed a renovation and addition project for the South Boston facility of electrical parts manufacturer Cole Hersee.

### Active in the Boston Community

CID Associates has been actively involved in the Greater Boston community through activities such as sponsoring the National Race for the Cure, which raises funds for breast cancer. The firm also supports the annual toothpick bridge competition for pre-engineering high school students held at Wentworth Institute.

For future projects, CID remains committed to its mission. "Our main thrust is to provide immediate, responsive service to the client," says King. "Our single source of accountability and expertise in the commercial industrial field is recognized, and we have been able to commit to projects and complete them within budget."

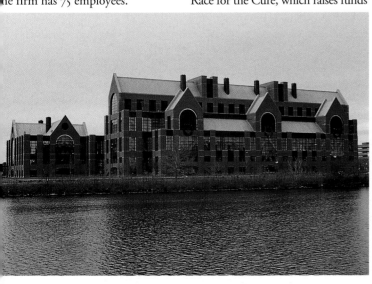

CID ASSOCIATES INC. PROVIDED STRUCTURAL ENGINEERING SERVICES FOR THE GENZYME MANUFACTURING FACILITY ON THE CHARLES RIVER AT ALLSTON LANDING IN BOSTON (LEFT).

IN 1992, CID ASSOCIATES INC. RECEIVED THE MASSACHUSETTS HISTORICAL COMMISSION'S PRESERVATION AWARD FOR ITS BUILDING ENVELOPE SERVICES AND HISTORIC RESTORATION OF THE WINTHROP BUILDING—OWNED BY FIDELITY INVESTMENTS—ON WATER STREET IN BOSTON'S FINANCIAL DISTRICT (RIGHT).

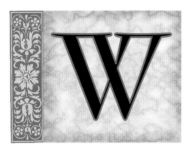

"W E HAD SPENT OUR LIVES BUILDING A REPUTATION O integrity, honesty, and quality, and we didn't want to los it," says Charles Raffi Jr., of the Wilmington, Delaware based Raffi and Swanson, Inc., a 70-year-old specialt chemicals and coatings company. The partners were startin to think about retirement, and with no heirs in sight, the

were looking for a buyer who would protect their life's work.

High Street Associates, Inc. met that need. High Street is a Boston-based acquisition and management company founded by a group of former Fortune 500 manufacturing executives, including Peter M. Jarowey, a former Cabot Corporation executive. The company specializes in acquiring and nurturing small and mid-sized, privately owned, family manufacturing businesses.

Typically, when a large company buys a smaller business, it recoups its investment by absorbing the

enterprise and cutting overhead— often by laying off staff. High Street takes a different approach, treating healthy small businesses as resources that can be developed with the assistance of broader experience and a different perspective. "The High Street Group is made up of builders who look at these companies as an opportunity for growth," says Walter Greeley, senior partner of High Street and a former Cabot Corporation executive vice president.

When High Street purchased Raffi and Swanson in 1990, the firm had been run since the 1950s

by Raffi and three other partners, all descendants of the company's founders. High Street worked to develop the business and, especially important for the owners, retained the 100-person workforce. Since then, sales have increased by more than 30 percent. "We are very pleased with High Street," says Raffi. "They've added some new thinking to the company."

**Building Sound Futures**

High Street Group was formed as an outgrowth of High Street Associates. Jarowey and his

THE HIGH STREET GROUP'S MOST RECENT ACQUISITION, CASTELLUCCI STONE INTERNATIONAL, IS ONE OF THE WORLD'S LARGEST ARCHITECTURAL GRANITE FABRICATORS AND QUARRIERS. THE COMPANY HAS PROVIDED THE STONE FOR NUMEROUS BUILDINGS, INCLUDING BOSTON'S SOUTH STATION.

partners set up the company to develop the value they saw in regionally focused, niche-oriented, private companies. Many of these businesses were successful and made money, but Jarowey thought they could benefit from the international experience and broadened perspective High Street Associates offered. "Some companies are not positioned well to effectively exploit their excellent products and ideas," he says. "We help change a company's perspective from a regional focus to one that will allow it to compete on a broader scale, perhaps in national and international markets."

Huntington Laboratories, Inc., a supplier of germicidal and antimicrobial products for the infection control market, was in a situation similar to Raffi and Swanson's when High Street Associates purchased the Indiana company in 1990. The founder's heirs were not interested in running the company, and

Huntington was looking for a buyer who would preserve its core values. High Street helped accelerate the company's product development, intensified its marketing effort, and introduced more detailed planning while leaving the staff intact. Since then, Huntington's business has increased more than 50 percent.

High Street's partners are skilled at turning a profit, but they emphasize that they are not financiers whose main function is to move money around. "We have found them to be individuals with expertise in building businesses, selecting market niches, and serving them well, while, at the same time, manufacturing high-quality, low-cost products and supporting them with excellent technical service," says Gerald Castellucci, vice president and general manager of High Street's most recent acquisition, Castellucci Stone International. One of the world's largest architectural granite fabricators and

quarriers, Castellucci Stone is located in Rhode Island. The company has provided the stone for high-visibility projects like Three and Four Times Square and the AT&T Building in New York City; Society Town in Cleveland, Ohio; and 500 Boylston Street in Boston. In addition, Castellucci Stone supplies overseas markets in Europe and Asia.

"They know what it is like to own and run a business," says Castelluci. "We appreciate their patience in helping us to rebuild and prosper, taking care to preserve and grow what our family spent four generations building."

The firm's commitment means that partnerships with High Street are win-win situations: High Street gains companies with proven track records and solid customer bases, while former owners rest assured that their companies, their employees, and their dreams will continue to prosper.

# Quebecor Printing (USA) Corp.

Q UEBECOR PRINTING (USA) CORP. IS TAKING THE TIME-HONORED centuries-old profession of printing and bringing it into the 21st century. As new and changing technologies have impacted the print industry, Quebecor's theme has been Turning Technology into Solutions. ❧ The second-largest commercial printer in the United States, Quebecor is driven by a companywide commit-

ment to quality and customer service, as well as to breaking new technological ground in the printing industry. Quebecor offers all the advantages of a global company, but with the personalized service of local operations. Its customers include many of the world's premier publishers, retailers, direct marketers, and other communications companies.

Headquartered in Boston, Quebecor Printing (USA) Corp. has nearly 50 printing and related services plants, with a similar number of close-to-the-customer sales offices. The company employs some 16,500 personnel, with locations in 30 U.S. states, plus Mexico. Annual sales exceed $2 billion, and the company is a wholly owned subsidiary of Montreal-based Quebecor Printing Inc., which owns more than 115 printing and related facilities throughout the world.

## A Decade of Growth

Quebecor Printing (USA) was born through a growth-by-acquisition strategy. The company was formed in 1990 to consolidate

Quebecor Printing Inc.'s U.S. operations after the acquisition of 14 printing plants from Graphics Holding Enterprises. Since then, the company has acquired numerous other printing plants and commercial printers. With strength in numbers, Quebecor Printing (USA) offers clients a single point of contact to the resources of a global graphic communications power: full services, diversified products, specialized facilities, extensive capacity, purchasing power, strong supplier contacts, advanced technology, and market leadership.

In addition to the corporate headquarters, Quebecor Printing (USA) has two operating facilities in Massachusetts: Quebecor Printing Eusey Press Inc. in Leominster, with a complementary specialty binding facility in West Bridgewater.

The company's nationwide operations are organized into product groups, which include Quebecor Magazines, Quebecor Books, Quebecor Catalogs, Quebecor Retail, Quebecor Direct, Quebecor Targeted Publications, Quebecor Integrated Media, and Quebecor Printing Directory Group. The service operations, which provide complementary services to the product groups, are Quebecor Imaging

Services, Quebecor Destination Services, and Quebecor List Services.

Customers include magazines such as *Time*, *Fortune*, *George*, and *People*; catalogs from Lillian Vernon and Sharper Image; book publishers Harcourt General, Addison Wesley Longman, and Houghton Mifflin; and retailers Sears, Macy's, and Filene's.

## A Full Range of Services

Quebecor's facilities offer extensive web-offset, gravure, sheetfed, and digital press capacity, complemented by the full range of print-related services. These include electronic prepress imaging, design, and photography; advanced ink-jet

imaging and selective binding; list and mailing services; continent-wide shipping and distribution; and electronic publishing and CD-ROM production and replications.

Dedicated to being a leading printer in the computer age, Quebecor has been an innovator in digital-based graphics, the direct digital and filmless process for gravure printing, and the deployment of computer-to-plate (CTP) systems that eliminate the film stage in offset printing.

Leading the way in digital demand printing, which prints and distributes books and fliers in a matter of minutes, Quebecor Printing (USA) initially developed a sophisticated digital print department at its Eusey Press facility in Leominster. Digital print equipment in other facilities in the United States and Canada allow for local and international digital print campaigns.

Along with innovation, the company is committed to quality. Quebecor is a leader in applying ISO 9000—the international quality standard—to the printing industry. The Eusey Press facility was one of the first commercial publication printers in the United States to become ISO 9000 registered.

## Combining Business with Responsibility

Quebecor believes that its sound business management is mutually compatible with a concern for the environment. As such, Quebecor initiated the ENVIRO-

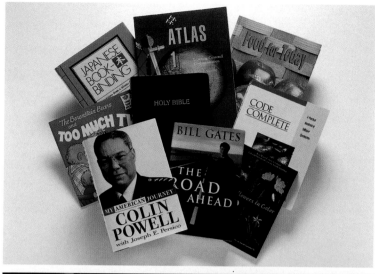

PRINTER program, a multifaceted approach to environmental responsibility, incorporating waste reduction, waste recovery, and recycling. Through this program, Quebecor works with clients, communities, governments, and industry to develop and promote environmentally sensitive printing practices. The company has successfully worked with major suppliers to develop more environmentally sensitive inks, papers, solvents, and other printing products.

Taking care of employees is also a priority for Quebecor. In 1999, the company introduced the Quebecor Printing Scholarship Program, which assists the dependents of Quebecor employees with the costs of higher education. In 1998, Quebecor founded a permanently endowed scholarship administered by the National Scholarship Trust Fund of the Graphic Arts. These awards are offered in addition to other scholarship opportunities

throughout the company for specific facilities or divisions.

Quebecor employees are at the heart of the company's integrated network of diversified but complementary printing and related graphic arts facilities. Combining the collective strengths of these operations and their employees, Quebecor Printing (USA) is equipped to take its global vision into the future.

**W**HEN PEOPLE THINK OF THE INTERNET, THE NAME CISCO Systems Inc. should come to mind. The high-tech company's routers, hubs, switches, and network management software—the off-ramps, interstate connectors, high-speed lanes, and traffic lights of the information superhighway—comprise the majority of the Internet's underpinnings. Through the company's prescient understanding of the wired world, combined with a savvy and aggressive business strategy, Cisco Systems is empowering the Internet generation and changing the way the world works, lives, learns, and plays in a positive way.

Cisco Systems burst onto the technology market scene in 1984, completed an initial public offering in 1990, and in 1996, achieved a $100 billion market capitalization after just 12 years in business, which is believed to be the fastest such acceleration ever. Measured by market capitalization, Cisco is the third-largest company traded on the Nasdaq stock exchange, and among the top 40 in the world. In fiscal year 1997, the company reported $6.33 billion in revenue. A global leader in networking for the Internet, Cisco holds the number one or number two market share in virtually every market segment in which it participates. Strategic acquisitions throughout the years have helped fuel Cisco's growth.

### The Networking Solution

**T**oday, Cisco provides its customers an end-to-end networking solution, meaning that Cisco offers one-stop shopping for all the hardware and software required to transmit data, voice, and video from a desktop, over a global network, and to its destination. Cisco's products include routers, local area network (LAN) and asynchronous transfer mode (ATM) switches, dial-up access servers, and network management software. These products, integrated by the Cisco IOS (internetwork operating system) network management software, link geographically dispersed networks to both private networks and the Internet.

Cisco serves customers in three markets: large organizations with complex networking needs, usually spanning multiple locations and types of computer systems; service providers, such as telecommunications carriers, Internet service providers, cable television companies, and wireless providers; and small and medium businesses with a need for data networks of their own, as well as a connection to their business partners and to the Internet.

Cisco, which sells its products in 90 countries, has more than 200 sales and support offices in 54 countries, and employs more than 14,000 people worldwide. Headquartered in San Jose, Cisco has major operations in Research Triangle Park, North Carolina, and Chelmsford, Massachusetts.

Massachusetts has been a location of recent expansion for Cisco. In August 1998, Cisco announced the opening of its New England Development Center in Chelmsford, an engineering and product development facility. The New England Development Center includes a newly leased building on Apollo Drive, as well as Cisco's original offices next door. Cisco also has a sales office

TAPPING INTO NEW ENGLAND'S WEALTH OF TALENT AND CREATIVITY, CISCO SYSTEMS INC. HAS ATTRACTED A TEAM OF HIGHLY SKILLED INDIVIDUALS WHO ENABLE THE COMPANY TO GROW.

on Hayden Avenue in Lexington. Cisco employs nearly 1,000 people throughout New England.

"New England has a wealth of talent and creativity," says Carl Redfield, senior vice president of manufacturing and senior executive for the New England Development Center. "We're here because the talent in New England will enable Cisco to grow. We're looking for the best in the industry. Having an operation in New England makes it easier to attract people who have roots here and who don't want to travel a long distance."

Cisco opened its New England operation in 1995, when it acquired the former Lightstream Inc. in Billerica. Other regional acquisitions include Littleton-based Nashoba Networks, and Summa Four Inc. of Manchester, New Hampshire, a leading provider of programmable switches. The Summa Four acquisition will help expand Cisco's network product line into the Internet telephony space. The company's other areas of expansion—particularly in New England—include the network transmission of cable and wireless technology.

With any new product line that Cisco develops, the company maintains its commitment to making customer service a priority, which Redfield says is a significant contributor to Cisco's success to date. Evidence of how serious the company is about customer satisfaction is the employee bonus program, which is closely linked to the results of an annual customer satisfaction survey. At Cisco, customer service is called customer advocacy, a philosophy instilled by one of Cisco's founders that affirms the need for customers to have advocates.

## The Importance of Education

Both in New England and on the national level, Cisco has contributed significant resources to advancing technology education. Nationally, Cisco's Networking Academies help high school and

college students develop practical networking knowledge and skills in a hands-on environment to prepare them for the Cisco Certified Network Associate exam. Cisco contributes curriculum development and program guidance, along with basic networking equipment to serve as a foundation for the school labs.

In Massachusetts, Cisco is a member of the Mass Networks Education Partnership, a collaborative effort to connect schools in Massachusetts by offering network design, equipment donations, and a volunteer initiative. The partnership

also focuses on curriculum reform and teacher-training programs that expand uses of educational technology in the classrooms.

At the University of Massachusetts-Lowell, Cisco awards two student scholarships each semester to the Colleges of Computer Science and Electrical Engineering. Cisco also offers advanced training courses to professors for curriculum development, and has donated both lab equipment and funds toward that effort.

In their dedication to furthering technology education, Cisco employees are acting as advocates for the Internet generation of the 21st century. "The people who work for Cisco are very much committed to advancing the state of the art in terms of the Internet economy," says Redfield. Wherever the next Internet generation goes, Cisco will provide much of the infrastructure.

A HOME AWAY FROM HOME IS WHAT BUSINESS AND LEISURE travelers find at the Embassy Suites hotel in Marlboro. Located at the "crossroads of New England" off Interstate 495 and minutes from the Massachusetts Turnpike, the Embassy Suites-Marlboro offers first-class service and a full range of amenities and recreational facilities, as well as state-of-the-art spaces for meetings,

conferences, and social functions. The upscale hotel opened its doors in July 1995, and two years later, it completed a $16 million renovation of the building that more than doubled the hotel's size to 229 suites from the original 100. The new, 129-suite building is adjoined to the original building, formerly a Quality Suites hotel, by a glass-enclosed atrium walkway. Situated within the six-story building is an elegant garden, complete with gazebo and pond. As part of the refurbishment, the hotel also renovated its four-story atrium, filled with trees and other foliage, along with Corcoran's Grill, the hotel's full-service restaurant and lounge. In addition, the hotel refurbished all of the original suites, upgrading bathrooms and adding new furniture and amenities.

## Matchless Amenities

For the leisure traveler, particularly those traveling with a family, the suites and hotel facilities offer something for everyone. Each suite features a private bedroom and living room. Also included are a refrigerator, wet bar, microwave, coffeemaker, hair dryer, and iron and ironing board, as well as two remote-control color televisions with movie and video game access, and two phones with voice messaging and data ports. The hotel also has 27 premium corner suites featuring full kitchens and marble fireplaces. These suites are perfect for the extended-stay traveler or honeymoon guests. The Embassy Suites-

Marlboro also provides an indoor swimming pool and sun deck, whirlpool, exercise equipment, game room, laundry services, and free parking, as well as complimentary access to a nearby full-service swim and racquet club.

Guest services are abundant at this Metro West hotel. Corcoran's Grill serves lunch and dinner daily. Suite service is also available for lunch and dinner. A complimentary, cooked-to-order American breakfast is served each morning in the garden atrium. And a hosted manager's reception each evening features free appetizers and nonalcoholic beverages. Other guest services include complimentary morning newspaper,

gift shop, guest laundry, valet service, express checkout, and safe-deposit boxes.

For the business traveler, the goal of Embassy Suites-Marlboro is to shorten the distance between work and relaxation. Every guest suite has built-in features and a well-lighted work space, providing an excellent small meeting room. In addition, the Embassy Suites-Marlboro offers a complete package of services for large meetings and conferences. The meeting areas include six rooms with 3,500 square feet of space, which can accommodate business meetings and social functions for groups of up to 50 people. Other amenities include a full-service business center, audio-visual equipment and services, and on-site catering.

Because Embassy Suites is dedicated to providing the finest in facilities and service to assure the quality and success of meetings and catered functions, the hotel offers its Meeting Guarantee, which pledges to fulfill the customer's requirements.

With its Metro West location, Embassy Suites-Marlboro offers travelers easy access to the surrounding cities of Boston, Cambridge, Worcester, and Providence. The hotel is just two miles from Compaq Computer and the Bell Atlantic Training Center; three miles from the New England Sports Center, .Com, and Fidelity Investments; five miles from Raytheon and Stratus; 4 miles from the Worcester Common Fashion Outlets; 26 miles from downtown Boston; 30 miles from

Harvard University; and 32 miles from Boston Logan International Airport. Shuttle service is available from both Logan Airport and Worcester Airport.

In the June 1998 issue of *Consumer Reports* magazine, the Embassy Suites chain was rated the number two upscale hotel behind Disney Resorts. Out of a possible 100 points, Embassy Suites scored 82.

### National Leader in All-Suites Hotels

Embassy Suites-Marlboro is part of the nation's leading chain of all-suite hotels, and is owned by the Memphis-based Promus Hotel Corporation, one of the world's largest hotel companies. Promus is the franchiser and operator of the Doubletree Hotels, Guest Suites and Resorts, Embassy Suites, Hampton Inn, Hampton Inn & Suites, Homewood Suites, Club Hotels by Doubletree, Embassy Vacation Resort, and Hampton Vacation Resort brands. A publicly traded company, Promus Hotel Corporation was created as a result of its 1995 spin-off from its former parent company, the Promus Companies Inc., and its subsequent December 1997 merger with Doubletree Corp. Promus has more than 1,275 hotels with more than 186,000 rooms, and approximately 40,000 employees throughout the United States, Canada, Mexico, and Central and South America.

There are 136 Embassy Suites hotels in the United States, Canada,

Latin America, and Asia. The Embassy Suites-Marlboro, which employs about 125 people, is the only Embassy Suites hotel in Massachusetts.

Since its arrival in the Metro West area, Embassy Suites-Marlboro has been an active community participant, with involvement in the Marlboro Chamber of Commerce and the charity events it sponsors. The hotel is also a corporate sponsor and donor to the Boys and Girls Club of Marlboro.

For all those traveling in the Metro West region, Embassy Suites-Marlboro—like all of the Embassy Suites hotels—goes the extra mile to live up to the chain's current slogan, What a difference a stay makes℠, with 100 percent satisfaction guaranteed.

THE WIRED AGE OF THE LATE 1990S MAY SOON BECOME AN anachronism, with wireless technology companies like Sprint PCS moving at supersonic speeds to untether individuals and businesses from traditional hardwired telephone lines. Improving upon first-generation analog cellular technology by building the second generation of wireless communications, Sprint PCS today has

the largest 100 percent digital, 100 percent PCS (personal communication services) nationwide wireless network in the United States.

Already serving more than 200 metropolitan markets that include more than 4,000 cities and communities across the country, Sprint PCS technology is based on CDMA (code division multiple access), an emerging standard in digital wireless technology. Independent testing has proved that CDMA technology offers superior clarity and security compared with analog cellular phones.

Headquartered in Kansas City, Missouri, Sprint PCS was launched in 1995 as a joint venture of Sprint Corp. and three cable television companies: Tele-Communications, Inc. (TCI), Cox Communications,

and Comcast Corp. The companies partnered to form the venture when the U.S. government auctioned off new FCC licenses for radio spectrum blocks. In the second round of government auctions that followed, Sprint PCS picked up more major markets, effectively gaining a license in every major market in America.

Sprint Corp. later purchased majority interest and operating control from its founding partners, and today, Sprint PCS is a subsidiary of Sprint Corp. More than 10,000 people are employed by Sprint PCS nationwide. Sprint PCS, together with its affiliates and Sprint Corp., has licensed PCS coverage of nearly 270 million people in all 50 states, Puerto Rico, and the U.S. Virgin Islands. Working with Sprint PCS in the design

and construction of this nationwide network are Lucent Technologies, Motorola, and Nortel.

### New England Expansion

In November 1997, just a few months after launching service in Greater Hartford, Sprint PCS expanded its network to Massachusetts and opened an office in Waltham, along the Route 128 Technology Highway. The company, which was the first digital wireless provider to launch in New England, moved quickly to expand its New England network. Today, the Sprint PCS network extends from southern Maine and New Hampshire, across Massachusetts, and throughout Rhode Island and Connecticut. Sprint PCS employs about 200 people throughout the New England region.

In Sprint PCS's rapid-fire U.S. rollout, New England was one of the last areas to have PCS service. Rolling terrain and heavy vegetation for six months of the year have posed unique engineering challenges. New England also has historic architecture and town commons dating back to colonial days, which many residents do not want to see juxtaposed with high-tech towers and facilities. Sprint PCS, sensitive to New England's desire to minimize any visual intrusion, has worked to create win-win partnerships with local towns and residents. More than two-thirds of the company's antennae in New England are located in churches, water towers, and other existing structures. As an example, Sprint PCS and the New Jerusalem Church in Bridgewater, Massachusetts, worked on a unique plan that benefited both parties.

A fire in 1994 severely damaged the historic church, built in 1871. In addition to interior water damage, the church's steeple and the roof

THROUGH ITS EDUCATION CONNECTION PROGRAM, SPRINT PCS DONATES WIRELESS PHONES AND SERVICE TO SCHOOLS SO THAT TEACHERS, COACHES, AND OTHER PERSONNEL ARE ONLY A PHONE CALL AWAY FROM PARENTS. HERE, TEACHER MARK SALZER AND STUDENT CAROLINE BRAXTER USE A SPRINT PCS WIRELESS PHONE AT THE MARY CURLEY MIDDLE SCHOOL IN BOSTON'S JAMAICA PLAIN NEIGHBORHOOD.

less Sprint PCS phones. Not only can school staff members receive parents' calls, but they also have a phone at their fingertips should they need to reach a parent quickly.

This shift in the way schools communicate is a precursor to the major shift in the way Americans will communicate in the near future. Sprint PCS already incorporates Caller ID, voice mail, short messaging, and other advanced features into its service. With its nationwide digital network and aggressive pricing structure, Sprint PCS envisions a day when wireless phones—initially adopted by the business user and affluent individuals—will become as common a communications vehicle as traditional phones are now.

Wireless technology has also emerged as a major safety enhancement. As part of its service, Sprint PCS offers a nationwide Roadside Rescue program. For roadside emergencies, customers enrolled in the program can access the service from their Sprint PCS phones, as well as via a toll-free number that can be dialed from any phone.

Sprint PCS, working with development partners Lucent Technologies, Motorola Cellular Infrastructure Group, Nortel, and Qualcomm, already has development plans under way for third-generation wireless systems based on the evolution of the cdmaOne™ standard. A leader in second-generation wireless technology, Sprint PCS is shaping the communications industry of the future.

f the sanctuary were destroyed. While insurance and fund-raising efforts enabled the church to rebuild the main structure, additional funds were needed for the steeple. Knowing that tall structures are appropriate for wireless phone antennae, the town approached Sprint PCS to see if the company would be willing to reconstruct the steeple and install its equipment inside. In late 1997, the church and Sprint PCS worked out just such an agreement. The $500,000 steeple restoration was completed in the fall of 1998.

## Education Connection

Sprint PCS is an active corporate citizen. Through its national Education Connection program, the firm donated wireless phones and services to the Fletcher School in Cambridge and the Mary Curley Middle School in Boston's Jamaica Plain neighborhood for use by teachers and administrators. Included in the donation were numerous Sprint PCS phones, which the schools can keep, and two years of free service.

The goal is to enhance communications among parents, teachers, and other school officials. Public schools typically have a limited number of telephone lines, which must accommodate the school's administrative telephone and fax use, plus classroom Internet access. This limited phone access often makes it difficult for teachers and parents to communicate in a timely manner during the school day. With the Education Connection program, classroom teachers, administrators, after-school coaches, and security personnel are always available to parents via their wire-

KARWAN PHOTOS

# Photographers

ERIC ANTONIOU, originally from Greece, attended the University of Massachusetts and the New England School of Photography. A self-employed photographer specializing in images of the performing arts, he has worked with clients such as the *Boston Globe* and *Boston Magazine*.

ANDREW BRILLIANT maintains a Boston-based commercial and editorial photo business and is also a scientific photographer at the Rosenstiel Basic Research Institute at Brandeis University. He has contributed to numerous publications, including *Newsweek*, *Life*, the *Boston Globe*, the *Los Angeles Times*, *Glamour*, and the *Boston Herald*. Brilliant's work has been exhibited in museums and galleries nationally, including the Museum of Modern Art in New York City.

KATHY CHAPMAN attended Minneapolis College of Art and Design and specializes in people, location, and music industry photography.

WEB CHAPPELL, originally from Bronxville, New York, has lived in Boston since 1982. He currently operates Web Chappell Photography, where he specializes in people and location photography. Chappell's work has also been featured in Towery Publishing's *Boston: Beacon for the New Horizon*.

DOUGLAS CHRISTIAN just completed photography for a book on the manufacture and trade of oriental rugs for Rizzoli International Publications. His client list includes Starbucks Corporation, AT&T, and Iris Graphics. Christian received a bachelor of fine arts degree from Tufts University.

KINDRA CLINEFF, a Midwesterner at heart, loves to photograph vineyards in Winchester and abroad. Her clients include the Massachusetts Office of Travel and Tourism, Michel Picard Vineyards, Vineyard Brands, and *Yankee*. Clineff moved to the Boston area in 1987.

JOHN D. CORNELIUS hails from Rochester, New York, and specializes in editorial, historical, and portrait photography.

MICHAEL R. DEMARCO is owner of Arts East, a service-oriented company specializing in art consultation and sales for commercial and residential clients. A graduate of the New England School of Photography's Professional Photography Program, he has amassed a clientele that includes Boston Harbor Hotel, Capellini's Restaurant, Covino Environmental Associates, and Faithful Church of Christ. DeMarco is a permanent exhibiting artist at the Vertu Fine Art Gallery in Newburyport and was featured in a solo show sponsored by the Newburyport Art Association.

TSAR FEDORSKY, a graduate of Amherst College, is owner of the Rockport-based Tsar Fedorsky Photography. Originally from New Orleans, he specializes in portraiture.

ERIC FOWKE specializes in environmental and portrait photography. A native of Medford, Massachusetts, he graduated from Salem State College.

TODD GIEG, a 16-year veteran freelance photographer, has been featured in numerous exhibitions and shows, most recently the group show *Naked and the Nude* at the New England School of Photography.

MIKE GREENLAR graduated from Rochester Institute of Technology (RIT) with a bachelor of arts degree in journalism. Currently self-employed and boasting seven years of newspaper experience, Greenlar has had images published in *Time*, *Newsweek*, *Life*, *Forbes*, *Fortune*, and *Business Week*, as well as Towery Publishing's *Greater Syracuse: Center of an Empire* and *Los Angeles: City of Dreams*. He specializes in editorial photography of people and technology, as well as contemporary images of Native Americans. In addition to giving frequent lectures at RIT, Greenlar has taught photojournalism at the S.I. Newhouse School of Public Communications.

JONATHAN HALBERG, born in Boston, has lived in Ohio, California, and Alabama, pursuing different careers in each state. Now a resident of Brookline, he is employed by AK Media/MA, and specializes in advertising, fashion, and sports photography.

BLAINE HARRINGTON III calls Colorado home when he is not traveling around the globe. For 10 weeks in the fall of 1996, he journeyed 36,000 air miles to 11 countries on photo shoots. In addition, he has contributed to a variety of magazines, including *Business Week*, *Forbes*, *Time*, *Newsweek*, *National Geographic Traveler*, and *Ski*. Harrington has worked assignments for the National Geographic Society and Time Life, and has taken cover photos for such travel guides as *Fodor's*, *Frommer's*, *Insight Guides*, and *Real Guides*. His photographs have also appeared in Towery Publishing's *Chicago: Heart and Soul of America*.

DAVID HENDERSON operates the Boston-based Henderson Studio, whose clients include Fidelity Investments, Hasbro, and *New Age Journal*. In his spare time, he enjoys woodworking, fly-fishing, and gardening.

HILLSTROM STOCK PHOTO, established in 1967, is a full-service stock photography agency based in Chicago. Its largest files include images of architecture, agriculture backgrounds, classic autos, gardens, and high-risk adventure/sports.

CAMI JOHNSON moved to the Boston area in 1991 from Alexandria, Virginia. She attended the New England School of Photography after graduating from Mary Washington College with a bachelor of science degree in psychology.

SUSAN COLE KELLY specializes "in illustrating the beauty of the vast American landscape in all its aspects, from life in our cities to wildlife in our national parks; from the intimate scope of a New England hill farm to the wide-open tundra of Alaska." After majoring in art at the University of New Hampshire, she studied at the New England School of Photography. Kelly, whose work has appeared in *Boston*, *Yankee*, *Down East Magazine*, *Historic Traveler*, and *Touring America*, is a member of the American Society of Media Photographers and a frequent contributor to *Yankee*'s Web site, www.newengland.com.

ASIA KEPKA attended the School of Theater Arts in Lodz in her native country of Poland before studying at the New England School of Photography. Her photographs have appeared in *Wired Magazine* and *Genzyme*, as well as on the album covers of Ani DiFranco's *Living in Clip* and *Little Plastic Castles*. Kepka's favorite photographic subjects are the elderly living in Eastern Europe.

JAMES LEAVITT received a bachelor of fine arts degree from Northeastern University. A self-employed photographer, his work has appeared in *Swing Magazine*, *FYI*, *Improper Bostonian*, and *Seafood Leader*.

BUD LEE studied at the Columbia University School of Fine Arts in New York and the National Academy of Fine Arts before moving to the Orlando area more than 20 years ago. A self-employed photojournalist, he founded both the Florida Photographers Workshop and the Iowa Photographers Workshop. Lee's work can be seen in *Esquire*, *Life*, *Travel & Leisure*, *Rolling Stone*, the *Washington Post*, and the *New York Times*, as well as in Towery Publishing's *Treasures on Tampa Bay: Tampa, St. Petersburg, Clearwater*; *Orlando: The City Beautiful*; *Jacksonville: Reflections of Excellence*; *Greater Syracuse: Center of an Empire*; and *Los Angeles: City of Dreams*.

JAMES LEMASS studied art in his native Ireland before moving to Cambridge, Massachusetts, in 1987. His areas of specialty include people and travel photography, and his work can be seen in publications by Aer Lingus, British Airways, and USAir, as well as the Nynex Yellow Pages. Lemass has also worked for the Massachusetts Office of Travel and Tourism, and his photographs have appeared in several other Towery publications, including *New York: Metropolis of the American Dream*; *Treasures on Tampa Bay: Tampa, St. Petersburg, Clearwater*; *Washington: City on a Hill*; *Orlando: The City Beautiful*; *San Diego: World-Class City*; *Los Angeles: City of Dreams*; and *Boston: Beacon for the New Horizon*.

LIZ LINDER's published works appear in a variety of media and marketing materials, including *Christian Science Monitor*, *Mix Magazine*, *Seventeen Magazine*, and *Rolling Stone*. She has amassed a clientele that includes Berklee College of Music, 20th Century Fox, Warner Bros., Massachusetts Institute of Technology, and Boston Center for the Arts. A graduate of Haverford College in Pennsylvania, Linder attended Bezalel Academy of Art and Design in Jerusalem, Israel.

STEVE LIPOFSKY, a lifelong resident of the Boston area, operates Lipofsky Photography. Specializing in sports images, he is the official photographer for the Boston Celtics and has contributed to *Sports Illustrated*, *Sport*, *Esquire*, and *Time*, as well as Towery Publishing's *Boston: Beacon for the New Horizon*. Lipofsky lives in Nahant, Massachusetts.

TIM LYNCH has photographed 40 states and 25 countries, and concentrates on capturing "real people" in his images. Originally from Rhode Island, he attended the New England School of Photography. Lynch specializes in corporate, sports, and digital photography.

KEN MARTIN, a member of the American Society of Picture Professionals, Liaison International, National Press Photographers Association, and Who's Who in Advertising, teaches photojournalism at Suffolk University in Boston. Through Kenneth Martin Photography/Amstock Photo, he focuses on Boston, New England, environmental issues, and corporate work. Martin's clients include Addison-Wesley Publishing, American Express Company, Children's Press, Sony Music Entertainment, and the *New York Times*. He lives in Bolton, Massachusetts, with his wife and son.

ADRIAN MILLER has traveled extensively throughout Europe and Asia. He graduated from the Public College of Engineering in Lucerne, Switzerland, with a major in constructional engineering and a minor in architectural photography. Miller placed first overall in the International Youth Hostel Photography Contest and won third place in the Light Sources/ Eastman Kodak Student Contest. He is currently studying photojournalism at the New England School of Photography.

METTE OTTOSSON, originally from Sweden, moved to Boston in 1996. A recent graduate of the New England School of Photography, she specializes in fashion images.

PHOTOPHILE, established in San Diego in 1967, is owned and operated by Nancy Likins-Mastern. An internationally known stock photography agency, the company houses more than 1 million color images, culled from more than 90 contributing local and international photographers. Photophile's 200-plus subject areas range from extensive coverage of the West Coast to business and industry, people and lifestyles, health, medicine, travel, scenic images, wildlife, and adventure sports.

CLARK QUIN, a graduate of the College of William and Mary and a self-taught photographer, operates the Boston-based Clark Quin Photography. While he specializes in advertising, corporate, and editorial assignments for clients such as Polaroid Corporation, New York Life, and *Wired*, Quin also devotes time to personal projects, including images of urban and natural environments, historical and undiscovered places, and funky Americana.

ANDREA RAYNOR attended the Maine College of Art and the School of Visual Arts in New York. Currently employed by the *Boston Phoenix*, her work has appeared in *Time Out*, the *Village Voice*, and *Boston Magazine*. Raynor is originally from Newtown, Connecticut.

ADELE ROTHMAN attended the New England School of Photography and received a bachelor of fine arts degree from Cornell University. Since graduating, she has established Adele Rothman Photography in Hyde Park and has joined the faculty of the New England School of Photography.

ANDY RYAN has amassed a clientele that includes BDM International, Boston Celtics, Parsons Brinkerhoff, *Scientific American*, *Boston Magazine*, *Condé Naste Traveler UK*, and *Food & Wine*. He has attended Fordham University, Boston College, and New York University's Tisch School of the Arts film school. In 1989, Ryan photographed the Tiananmen Square massacre in Beijing, China. A Boston native, he is involved in a long-term documentary project studying the effects of the Gulf War and subsequent sanctions on the civilian population of Iraq.

STEPHEN SETTE-DUCATI is the sole proprietor of Sette-Ducati Photographic, an architectural photography-based business. His client list includes CMI Healthcare, Bierly-Drake Associates, *Design Times* magazine, EGA Architects, and Uno Restaurant Corporation. After graduating from Wentworth Institute of Technology with a degree in interior design, Sette-Ducati studied at the Art Institute of Boston.

WALTER SILVER received a Kodak Brownie camera from his father at the age of four and has been making photographs ever since. During his professional career he has enjoyed hanging out of helicopters, crawling on the floor with preschoolers, making mundane factories look like art and prosaic processes look elegant, and trying not to faint during medical procedures. An 18-year veteran freelance photographer, Silver serves a client list that includes Boston Scientific Corporation, Bright Horizons Family Solutions, The Gillette Company, Medtronic, and Reebok International.

ETER SIMON's work has appeared in a variety of print media includ-
ing *Time, Newsweek, People,* the *Village Voice, Boston Magazine, New
York Magazine,* the *New York Times,* and *Rolling Stone.* He has had
one-man shows at the Nikon House and Niekrug Gallery in New
York, and the Kiva Gallery in Boston. Simon has lived on Martha's
Vineyard since 1973.

ANA SMITH, a native of New Bedford, Massachusetts, enjoys editorial
photography and photojournalism. A graduate of Boston's New England School of Photography, Smith's work has appeared in *Yankee,
U.S. News & World Report, Entertainment Weekly, People, Time, Fortune,* and *Money,* as well as in Towery Publishing's *Providence: A
Rhode Island Mosaic.*

ANDY SNOW is a photographer who has lived and worked in southwestern Ohio for more than 25 years. While he specializes in corporate
and editorial photography, his true passion is environmental portraiture. Snow's clients include General Electric, Cincinnati Bell, AT&T,
Mead, *Time, Forbes, Fortune,* and *Business Week.* He is the author and
photographer of *Location Photography Secrets: How to Get the Right
Shot Every Time.*

AREN SPARACIO, originally from Vineland, New Jersey, specializes in
photojournalism and documentary photography. After receiving a bach-
lor of arts degree from Rutgers College, she studied at the New England
School of Photography.

BRIAN WALSKI is employed by the *Los Angeles Times* as a photojournalist. While at the Boston Herald, he has covered many major stories
including the Gulf War, the famine in Somalia, and the conflicts in
Northern Ireland and the Indian State of Kashmir. Walski was born in
Illinois, grew up in Chicago, and studied journalism at Northern Illinois University.

Additional photographers and organizations that contributed to *Boston:
History in the Making* include Allsport Photography USA Inc.; the
Bostonian Society; Corbis-Westlight; Folio, Inc.; Mark Ostow; Greg
Probst; and Eric Roth.

Printed in Canada

Copyright © 1999 by Towery Publishing, Inc.
All rights reserved. No part of this work may be reproduced or copied in
any form or by any means, except for brief excerpts in conjunction with
book reviews, without prior written permission of the publisher.

Towery Publishing, Inc., The Towery Building, 1835 Union Avenue,
Memphis, TN 38104

PUBLISHER: J. Robert Towery
EXECUTIVE PUBLISHER: Jenny McDowell
ASSOCIATE PUBLISHER: Michael C. James
NATIONAL SALES MANAGER: Stephen Hung
MARKETING DIRECTOR: Carol Culpepper
PROJECT DIRECTORS: Mary Whelan, Paul Withington, Mary Hanley, Phil
    Hernberg, Richard Jones
EXECUTIVE EDITOR: David B. Dawson
MANAGING EDITOR: Lynn Conlee
SENIOR EDITOR: Carlisle Hacker
EDITOR/PROFILE MANAGER: Mary Jane Adams
EDITORS: Jana Files, John Floyd, Heather Ramsey, Brian Johnston
ASSISTANT EDITOR: Rebecca Green
EDITORIAL ASSISTANT: Sunni Thompson
PROFILE WRITERS: Colleen Frye, Charles E. Vermette
CAPTION WRITER: David Blair
CREATIVE DIRECTOR: Brian Groppe
PHOTOGRAPHY EDITOR: Jonathan Postal
PHOTOGRAPHIC CONSULTANTS: Christine Car and Joseph Heroun
PHOTOGRAPHY COORDINATOR: Robin McGehee
PROFILE DESIGNERS: Laurie Beck, Kelley Pratt, Ann Ward
PRODUCTION RESOURCES MANAGER: Dave Dunlap Jr.
PRODUCTION COORDINATOR: Brenda Pattat
PRODUCTION ASSISTANTS: Loretta Drew, Melissa Ellis
DIGITAL COLOR SUPERVISOR: Darin Ipema
DIGITAL COLOR TECHNICIANS: Eric Friedl, Brent Salazar
PRINT COORDINATOR: Tonda Thomas

LIBRARY OF CONGRESS CATALOGING-IN-PUBLICATION DATA

Parker, Robert B., 1932-
    Boston : history in the making / by Robert B. Parker ;  art
direction by Jil Foutch.
        p.   cm. — (Urban tapestry series)
    Includes index.
    ISBN 1-881096-66-1 (alk. paper)
    1. Boston (Mass.)—Civilization.  2. Boston (Mass.)—Pictorial
works.  3. Boston (Mass.)—Economic conditions.  4. Business
enterprises—Massachusetts—Boston.  I. Title.  II. Series.
F73.52.P37  1999
974.4'61—dc21                                          99-19132

TIP T TOMATO
GATES BROS.

# Index of Profiles